I0460385

SIXTY COMEDY DUET SCENES FOR TEENS

LAURIE ALLEN

Real-life situations for laughter

MERIWETHER PUBLISHING LTD.
Colorado Springs, Colorado

Meriwether Publishing Ltd., Publisher
PO Box 7710
Colorado Springs, CO 80933-7710

Editor: Arthur L. Zapel
Assistant editor: Audrey Scheck
Cover design: Jan Melvin

© Copyright MMVIII Meriwether Publishing Ltd.
Printed in the United States of America
First Edition

Library of Congress Cataloging-in-Publication Data

Allen, Laurie, 1962-
  Sixty comedy duet scenes for teens : real-life situations for laughter / by Laurie Allen
    p. cm.
  ISBN 978-1-56608-152-8 (pbk.)
  1. Young adult drama, American. I. Title.
PS3601.L4324S59   2008
812'.04108--dc22

                              2007043506

            1   2   3   08   09   10

Dedication

To Dawn, my best friend at Snyder High School,
for the laughter we shared, crazy ideas we acted out on,
wide-eyed looks no one understood, secrets kept,
dreams revealed, getting caught,
and getting away with all those things we'll never forget!

Table of Contents

About the Author

Preface

In high school, life was an adventure filled with zany situations and laughter as my girlfriend and I acted out our next so-called great idea. Most of the time we found ourselves laughing as we faced life with an unstoppable attitude. Drawing from those experiences, I have created these comedy duet scenes which take place within the confines of school. You will find the characters are daring, outlandish, uninhibited, and creative as they deal with their circumstances that are often exaggerated by their own attitudes, perceptions, and actions. Teen actors will easily identify with the believable characters that focus on subjects they can easily relate to such as dating, appearances, egos, fads, crushes, breaking rules, broken hearts, failing grades, classroom assignments, embarrassing moments, the over-enthusiastic teacher, and more. Their peers will laugh out loud as they watch these realistic scenes emerge in a humorous way.

These duets may be performed by middle school or high school students and are appropriate for all ages. The simple sets and few props make staging quite simple. They are perfect for classroom practice or for an evening of entertainment. Teens will not only enjoy reading these scenes but will be anxious to jump up and perform these comical situations as they show off their talents.

— Laurie Allen

Two Women

1. Vote for Me

Cast: MEG, KATIE
Props: Poster board.
Setting: School hallway.

1   *(AT RISE: MEG is holding a large poster board, which reads:*
2   *"VOTE FOR ME!" KATIE enters and MEG enthusiastically*
3   *jumps in front of her.)*
4   **MEG:** Vote for me!
5   **KATIE:** For what?
6   **MEG:** Most popular girl in the junior class! They're having
7   elections on Friday, so I'm out campaigning. *(Waving the*
8   *sign)* Vote for me!
9   **KATIE:** Uh ... shouldn't you have put your name on that sign?
10 **MEG:** Oh, I don't need to do that. Everyone knows me!
11 **KATIE:** I don't know you.
12 **MEG:** You don't? Then you must be a new student, right?
13 **KATIE:** No.
14 **MEG:** Then you have to know me! Everyone knows me!
15 **KATIE:** I don't know you.
16 **MEG:** How is that possible? Do you live in a bubble?
17 **KATIE:** Look, I have a lot of friends. I guess we just don't run in
18   the same crowd.
19 **MEG:** I guess. Hey, do you know Brooke Taylor?
20 **KATIE:** Brooke Taylor? Of course I know Brooke Taylor! She's
21   practically my best friend!
22 **MEG:** What? But ... Brooke Taylor is *my* best friend!
23 **KATIE:** Are you serious? Wow. And we had lunch together
24   today.
25 **MEG:** You did? This is too weird! Brooke and I have been
26   friends since the first grade. In elementary we walked

1   home together from school every day. And in junior high
2   we took the same bus. Of course, now that we have cars we
3   do our own thing, but we still hang out.

4   KATIE: Wow. And to think we never met.

5   MEG: Hey, do you know Ryan Foster?

6   KATIE: Ryan Foster? Oh, of course I know him! Ryan and I are
7   like this! *(Crosses fingers to demonstrate.)*

8   MEG: Oh, really? Well, Ryan is *my* boyfriend!

9   KATIE: *(Uncrosses fingers)* Ryan is *your* boyfriend?

10   MEG: Six months, going on seven!

11   KATIE: Wow. I didn't know that.

12   MEG: And you and Ryan are like this? *(Crosses fingers.)*

13   KATIE: Oh, well, uh ... Just at school. We have a couple of classes
14   together.

15   MEG: But ... Ryan and I have a couple of classes together, too.
16   This is really strange.

17   KATIE: Yes, very.

18   MEG: So, do you happen to know Allison Sawyer?

19   KATIE: Oh, of course! Who doesn't know Allison Sawyer? In
20   fact, I spent the night at her house last weekend.

21   MEG: You did?

22   KATIE: Uh-huh. So, how do you know Allison?

23   MEG: Allison Sawyer is *my* cousin!

24   KATIE: Wow. It really is a small world. Well, kind of. Except for
25   the fact that you and I don't know each other.

26   MEG: This just doesn't make any sense. I'm, like, the most out-
27   going, most friendly, most fun, and most popular person
28   in school. How is it possible that you don't know me?

29   KATIE: Well, I could ask you the same question. How is it
30   possible that you don't know me? I'm the President of the
31   French Club, a member of the Academic Decathlon,
32   Secretary for the Future Leaders of America, a member of
33   the Pep Squad, in Drama, Choir, Orchestra ... What do you
34   do?

35   MEG: Well, I ... I, uh ... I'm a teacher's aide for Mrs. Hamilton.

1   **KATIE: But what clubs do you belong to?**

2   **MEG: Look, I'm too busy socializing with all my friends to have**

3   **time to be in any clubs.**

4   **KATIE: Are you in the band?**

5   **MEG: No.**

6   **KATIE: On the Yearbook Committee?**

7   **MEG: No.**

8   **KATIE: Play sports?**

9   **MEG: Look, I told you, I socialize.**

10 **KATIE: But you're not in any clubs or organizations?**

11 **MEG: No, I don't have time for any of that. My social life is way**

12   **too busy!**

13 **KATIE: But what about academics? Are you in the top ten?**

14 **MEG: No, I wouldn't say I'm the smartest. But, I'm in the top**

15   **ten as far as popularity goes!** *(Points to sign.)*

16 **KATIE: Oh. Well, sorry I don't know you. And I'm sure you're a**

17   **lot of fun to hang out with.**

18 **MEG: I am. And you** *really* **don't know who I am?**

19 **KATIE: No. Sorry.**

20 **MEG: Well, you do now!**

21 **KATIE: You're right.**

22 **MEG: So now you can vote for me!** *(Shakes sign.)*

23 **KATIE: And I will. I really will.**

24 **MEG: Thanks. I appreciate it. Well, I better go now and round**

25   **up some more votes.**

26 **KATIE: Good luck.**

27 **MEG: Thanks. And don't forget ... Vote for me!**

28 **KATIE: I won't forget!** *(MEG exits.)* **Oh no! I forgot to get her**

29   **name!**

2. Dear Santa

Cast: ALYSSA, MONICA

Props: Paper, pen.

Setting: A classroom.

1   *(AT RISE: ALYSSA and MONICA are sitting at their desks.)*
2   **ALYSSA:** *(Leans over to MONICA.)* **Are we in kindergarten?**
3   **MONICA: Obviously Mrs. Owens thinks so!**
4   **ALYSSA: Has she lost her mind?**
5   **MONICA: It appears that way.**
6   **ALYSSA: And have you noticed? Everyone except for us is**
7   **getting into this writing assignment. "Dear Santa, all I**
8   **want for Christmas is ..."**
9   **MONICA: My two front teeth!**
10   **ALYSSA: Why is she making us do this? I mean, it'd be OK if we**
11   **were five years old!**
12   **MONICA: Maybe there's a point to this and she'll explain later.**
13   **ALYSSA: And in the meantime, we have to write a letter to jolly**
14   **old Saint Nick!** *(Writes.)* **"Dear Santa ..."** *(Taps her pen on*
15   *her desk as she thinks.)* **"Dear Santa ..." Monica, why am I**
16   **writing to someone who doesn't exist?**
17   **MONICA: Because Mrs. Owens said we have to! No explanation**
18   **as to why, but just that it would count as a major grade!**
19   **Writing Santa is a major grade. Please! This is ridiculous!**
20   **ALYSSA: Dear Santa ... I don't believe in you! Stopped believing**
21   **in you that year you didn't bring me a horse! Because**
22   **that's all my little heart desired was a horse! But noooo!**
23   **MONICA: Dear Santa, all I want for Christmas it for Joey**
24   **McAdams to ask me out.**
25   **ALYSSA: And I'll take a shiny new Corvette, thank you very**
26   **much.**

1   MONICA: And a play station.

2   ALYSSA: And a new iPod.

3   MONICA: New computer.

4   ALYSSA: And money. Lots and lots of money.

5   MONICA: Yeah! Let's ask dear old Santa for a million bucks
6   each.

7   ALYSSA: Let's make it two. A million dollars doesn't go as far as
8   it used to.

9   MONICA: *(Writing)* "Dear Santa, all I want for Christmas is two
10   million dollars."

11   ALYSSA: That's what I'm writing, too.

12   MONICA: Finished!

13   ALYSSA: Me too. *(They look around the room.)* Did we miss
14   something? Everyone else is still writing.

15   MONICA: Probably because they're naming off all the things
16   they want for Christmas. But we were smart. We just
17   asked for money.

18   ALYSSA: *(Smiles.)* Two million dollars. I wish.

19   MONICA: You know, Alyssa, we've only written one sentence.
20   And this is for a major grade.

21   ALYSSA: Hey, we wrote to Santa. We told him what we wanted.
22   How can we get a failing grade for that?

23   MONICA: But one sentence? I'm sure Mrs. Owens is looking for
24   a little more creativity here.

25   ALYSSA: You're right. She'll probably give us a zero for lack of
26   effort. Great! A zero for a crappy letter to Santa Claus!

27   MONICA: This is stupid!

28   ALYSSA: OK, something longer, something more creative ...

29   MONICA: I bet everyone else is asking for something less
30   selfish like world peace.

31   ALYSSA: That's stupid! Santa doesn't provide world peace!

32   MONICA: Or for all the hungry children in the world to be fed.

33   ALYSSA: Santa can't do that!

34   MONICA: I don't think he can bring us a million dollars, either.

35   ALYSSA: Two million, remember?

1   MONICA: So what should was ask for?

2   ALYSSA: Toys, I guess.

3   MONICA: *(Writing)* "Dear Santa, all I want for Christmas is a

4   forty-two-inch, high-definition plasma TV for my room."

5   *(Pauses as she thinks.)* "And peace on earth and good will

6   towards men."

7   ALYSSA: *(Writing)* I'll take one of those. And a puppy!

8   MONICA: A puppy?

9   ALYSSA: Hey, maybe that horse was too big for his sleigh. So if

10   Santa is real, surely he can manage a puppy! *(Pause, then*

11   *writes.)* "And the eradication of world hunger."

12   MONICA: That sounded intelligent.

13   ALYSSA: Thank you. I'm finished.

14   MONICA: Me too. *(Pause.)* "P.S. And will you please quit teasing

15   kids into thinking you are real?"

16   ALYSSA: *(Writes.)* "Because I don't believe in you!"

17   MONICA: *(Writes.)* "And I don't believe in you!"

18   ALYSSA: *(Writes.)* "So why don't you just go jump in a lake?"

19   MONICA: *(Writes.)* "Because you're a fat ugly slob!"

20   ALYSSA: *(Writes.)* "And you need a new outfit!"

21   MONICA: *(Writes.)* "And you need to go on a diet! Stop eating all

22   those cookies!"

23   ALYSSA: *(Writes.)* "And get a makeover!"

24   MONICA: *(Writes.)* "Lose the stupid glasses!"

25   ALYSSA: *(Writes.)* "Try contacts!"

26   MONICA: *(Writes.)* "And stop saying 'ho, ho, ho,' because it's

27   getting on our nerves!"

28   ALYSSA: *(Looks up.)* Did you hear that? Mrs. Owens wants us to

29   turn in our papers now.

30   MONICA: Uh-oh.

31   ALYSSA: I'll do it. *(Takes the papers, exits, then quickly returns.)*

32   I have some bad news.

33   MONICA: What?

34   ALYSSA: Mrs. Owens said that not only is this assignment for a

35   major grade, but our letters are going to be printed in the

1   local newspaper on Christmas Eve.

2 MONICA: What? But we called Santa Claus a fat, ugly slob!

3 ALYSSA: And told him to go jump in a lake.

4 MONICA: This is bad.

5 ALYSSA: Bad? It's a disaster! Not only are we going to get a
6   failing grade, but to top that off, we will be publicly
7   humiliated!

8 MONICA: Alyssa, do you think there's a chance we can get our
9   papers back? Tell Mrs. Owens we want to add a couple
10   more things?

11 ALYSSA: I don't know, but we better try! *(They jump up and exit.)*

3. Ugly Debbie

Cast: NICOLE, DEBBIE
Props: Large black glasses.

1   *(AT RISE: DEBBIE, wearing glasses, sits at a table reading.*
2   *NICOLE enters.)*
3   **NICOLE: Debbie, you got glasses!**
4   **DEBBIE: Yeah. So tell me, what do you think?**
5   **NICOLE:** *(Trying to sound optimistic)* **Well, they, uh ... make you**
6   **look ... you know ... smart.**
7   **DEBBIE: But I don't want to look smart. I want to look cute.**
8   **NICOLE: You are, but ... aren't those glasses just a little bit too**
9   **big for your face? I mean, did you look at any of those**
10   **small, narrow styles?**
11   **DEBBIE: These are the ones I liked. Don't you like them?**
12   **NICOLE: Sure. But, uh ... did you ever think about wearing**
13   **contacts?**
14   **DEBBIE: I tried contacts, but they didn't work.**
15   **NICOLE: Why not? Do you have astigmatism?**
16   **DEBBIE: No, but I have a fear of sticking a foreign object into**
17   **my eye.**
18   **NICOLE: Oh.**
19   **DEBBIE: Tomorrow I'm getting braces, too. Do you think I'll**
20   **still look cute then?**
21   **NICOLE: Braces, too?**
22   **DEBBIE: Uh-huh.**
23   **NICOLE: But why?**
24   **DEBBIE: Because my teeth are crooked! Why else? See.** *(Gives*
25   *her a wide smile.)*
26   **NICOLE: But most people get braces in junior high. Not high**
27   **school.**

1 DEBBIE: I know, but my mouth wasn't ready for them until
2   now. My mom said I didn't cut my first tooth until I was a
3   year old. Guess I'm a late bloomer.
4 NICOLE: You could always get those clear braces.
5 DEBBIE: Unfortunately they're too expensive. I have to get
6   those silver ones.
7 NICOLE: Oh, yuck!
8 DEBBIE: Yuck?
9 NICOLE: I mean ... you know ...
10 DEBBIE: But the good part about it is that I'm going to get
11   those colored bands on my braces. That'll be cool, huh?
12 NICOLE: I guess. What color?
13 DEBBIE: Bright green!
14 NICOLE: Bright green? Are you sure? Bright green?
15 DEBBIE: I love that color! *(A wide smile as she talks)* I think it'll
16   be cute, don't you?
17 NICOLE: But aren't you afraid it'll look like you have broccoli
18   stuck in your teeth?
19 DEBBIE: No! Those colored bands are what make braces fun to
20   wear.
21 NICOLE: I guess. But bright green? Are you sure?
22 DEBBIE: Yes! I love green!
23 NICOLE: Wow. So, glasses and braces all in the same week.
24   You'll definitely look, you know ... different.
25 DEBBIE: Ugly?
26 NICOLE: I didn't say ugly.
27 DEBBIE: You didn't say cute! So it's true! I'm going to be ugly!
28   I'm going to be the ugliest girl in high school!
29 NICOLE: No, no ...
30 DEBBIE: Yes I am!
31 NICOLE: No, Debbie.
32 DEBBIE: Then name someone who will be uglier than me!
33 NICOLE: OK. *(Long pause.)*
34 DEBBIE: See!
35 NICOLE: I was thinking! *(Pause.)*

1   **DEBBIE:** Because you can't think of anyone!

2   **NICOLE:** I know!

3   **DEBBIE:** Who?

4   **NICOLE:** Bobwinna Newby!

5   **DEBBIE:** Bobwinna Newby?! Gee thanks, Nicole! And that's

6   only because she has glasses, braces, *and pimples*! And on

7   a bad week, we'll probably be tied for the ugly girl prize.

8   So, this is just great! Me and Bobwinna Newby, the two

9   ugliest girls at school!

10 **NICOLE:** Debbie, it's only temporary! I mean, by the time you

11   get out of high school, your teeth will be perfectly straight,

12   and you'll probably find the courage to put those contacts

13   into your eyes. So then you'll practically be Miss America!

14 **DEBBIE:** And until then?

15 **NICOLE:** Until then ... well, you just hold your head up high!

16 **DEBBIE:** Don't you think I should do the opposite? You know,

17   look down so no one will be grossed out?

18 **NICOLE:** That's ridiculous. You're not going to be *that* ugly.

19 **DEBBIE:** *That* ugly? What are you saying? I'll be a little ugly? Or

20   is that a lot ugly? Nicole, I don't want to be ugly at all! I

21   want to be cute!

22 **NICOLE:** And you will be!

23 **DEBBIE:** That's right! Just as soon as I convince my mom to let

24   me get my lip, nose, and eyebrow pierced!

25 **NICOLE:** What?

26 **DEBBIE:** Then I'll look hot!

27 **NICOLE:** You'd actually do that?

28 **DEBBIE:** In a heartbeat!

29 **NICOLE:** Pierce your lip, nose, and eyebrow? All three?

30 **DEBBIE:** Then who's going to notice my stupid glasses and

31   braces? So instead of being Ugly Debbie, I'll be the hippest

32   and hottest chick you've ever seen!

33 **NICOLE:** But ... I thought you wanted to go for cute!

34 **DEBBIE:** Cute is overrated, don't you think? Wouldn't you

35   rather be hot?

1   NICOLE: Let me picture this. Glasses. Braces with bright green
2   bands. Plus, your lip, nose, and eyebrow pierced.
3   DEBBIE: Yes!
4   NICOLE: Wow. You won't even look the same.
5   DEBBIE: Bobwinna Newby will be the ugliest girl then! Even if
6   I get a few pimples, she still won't compare to me!
7   NICOLE: No ...
8   DEBBIE: Then I'll be hot!
9   NICOLE: *(Trying to agree)* Uh, yeah.

4. My Mom Is My Teacher

Cast: LISA, MOM
Props: Paper.
Setting: A classroom.

1 *(AT RISE: MOM is preparing her classroom for the first day of*
2 *class.)*
3 **LISA:** Here's the deal, Mom. I don't want anyone finding out
4 that you're my mom.
5 **MOM:** But sweetheart, all your friends know that I'm your
6 mom. So, what's the problem?
7 **LISA:** They can keep it a secret. Can you?
8 **MOM:** You're being silly.
9 **LISA:** Mom, listen! Just treat me like any of your other
10 students, OK?
11 **MOM:** All right. That won't be a problem.
12 **LISA:** And I'll call you Mrs. Smith, OK?
13 **MOM:** That's fine. But don't be expecting any favors from
14 me.
15 **LISA:** What do you mean?
16 **MOM:** Well, don't expect me to give you a passing grade just
17 because you're my daughter.
18 **LISA:** *(Laughs.)* Mom, you wouldn't fail me.
19 **MOM:** If you don't do your assignments and pass the tests,
20 then yes, I'll fail you.
21 **LISA:** But what if I need some extra help? You'll give that to
22 me, won't you?
23 **MOM:** Of course.
24 **LISA:** And maybe some answers, too?

1   MOM: No, Lisa. You'll have to work just as hard as everyone
2   else in this class. Maybe even harder.
3   LISA: But Mom, you know I hate Chemistry. In fact, I hate it
4   so much that I don't even know how we could be
5   related.
6   MOM: If you study, you'll do fine.
7   LISA: But what if it's too hard for me? What if it just doesn't
8   sink in? Wouldn't you help me out? Like maybe give me
9   a little extra credit?
10 MOM: No, Lisa. No extra credit. But I do provide tutoring at
11   seven a.m. every Monday, Wednesday, and Friday.
12 LISA: But Mom, can't you tutor me at home after dinner?
13   Because you know I detest mornings!
14 MOM: Lisa, if I'm going to treat you like everyone else, then
15   you'll do as everyone else. Tutoring is at seven a.m.
16 LISA: Gee, thanks, Mom.
17 MOM: Lisa, why are you so worried? You make good grades.
18 LISA: Because I've heard about Mrs. Smith's Chemistry
19   class!
20 MOM: Oh really? And what have you heard?
21 LISA: Mom, I'm sorry, but everyone hates your class! It's too
22   hard.
23 MOM: Only to those students who don't pay attention.
24 LISA: Mom, have you ever noticed how a lot of students have
25   to take your class twice?
26 MOM: Only because they didn't pay attention the first time.
27 LISA: Maybe because you move along too fast.
28 MOM: No, I don't think so.
29 LISA: Or maybe you need to make it more interesting. You
30   know, like using games and prizes for correct answers.
31 MOM: My prize for correct answers is a passing grade. No
32   games.
33 LISA: Or how about letting us watch movies on Fridays! Not
34   a chemistry movie, but a movie everyone likes. Like ...
35   like *Terror of the Walking Dead*. That'd be fun!

1   MOM: Tests are on Fridays. No exceptions.
2   LISA: Then what about having an open-book test? A lot of
3   teachers do that nowadays.
4   MOM: Now, explain that to me. How is it a test if you can
5   open your book and find the answers?
6   LISA: It's a test to see if you can find the right answers! And
7   when you do, you're learning as you copy the answers
8   onto your test.
9   MOM: *(Laughs.)* No, sorry. I don't allow open-book tests in
10   my class. In fact, I have all the students stack their
11   textbooks on top of the table before we begin.
12   LISA: Would you ever allow one index card of notes to be
13   used for a test?
14   MOM: No. *(Taps head.)* You have to have it up here!
15   LISA: Great!
16   MOM: I have an idea!
17   LISA: What?
18   MOM: Well, if you want to get a head start on my Chemistry
19   class, you could start memorizing the Periodic Table of
20   Elements. And just to show you how helpful I can be,
21   here's a study sheet for our first quiz next week on
22   chemical bonds and compounds. *(Offers her the paper.)*
23   LISA: Mom, no!
24   MOM: I'm just trying to help.
25   LISA: No, thanks. I'll just struggle along with everyone else!
26   MOM: Well, this could be fun.
27   LISA: What? Pretending that we don't know each other?
28   MOM: Talking about my class every night over dinner. We
29   can talk about what we studied that day. I could give
30   you a little review. Maybe a pop quiz over dessert ...
31   LISA: A pop quiz over dessert? Mom!
32   MOM: You could tell me what the students thought about
33   the class ...
34   LISA: Mom, I can tell you right now! They hate your class!
35   MOM: But it hasn't even started.

1 LISA: Word gets around. And mom, everyone hates
2   Chemistry. Especially me, your own daughter!
3 MOM: Well, daughter, you will have to pass my class, just
4   like everyone else.
5 LISA: And if I slip up and call you Mom, just ignore me, OK?
6 MOM: And if I slip and call you my daughter, well, you better
7   not ignore me. *(Laughs.)*
8 LISA: *(Turns to exit.)* I'm going home now, *Mrs. Smith*!
9 MOM: Oh, it'll be fun. You'll see. *(Hollering)* Oh, and Lisa,
10   when you get home, please pick your clothes up from
11   the bathroom floor.
12 LISA: *(Turns.)* Mom, never, and I mean never tell me that
13   stuff during class, OK?
14 MOM: What? That I hate it when you leave your
15   undergarments all over the bathroom floor?
16 LISA: Mom! Remember! You don't know me and I don't
17   know you! And most importantly, I'm not your
18   daughter!
19 MOM: Well, that's going to be hard to forget!
20 LISA: Mom!
21 MOM: Don't you mean Mrs. Smith? *(LISA screams and exits.)*

5. Not the Next Cheerleader

Cast: KATHY, LAURA
Setting: Gym.

1 KATHY: Laura, guess what? I've decided to try out for
2   cheerleader! So, tell me, what do you think of this
3   jump? *(Does an awkward and clumsy jump.)*
4 LAURA: Wow. That was, uh ...
5 KATHY: Or how about this one? *(Does another bad jump.)* Do
6   you like it better than the first one?
7 LAURA: Uh ... I'm not sure.
8 KATHY: And, get this, I've invented my own cheer!
9   *(Demonstrates.)* "We are, we are, we are the Tigers! We
10   are, we are, we are the Tigers! Go! Fight! Win!" *(Finishes*
11   *with another awkward jump.)* What do you think? Good,
12   huh?
13 LAURA: Honestly?
14 KATHY: Honestly.
15 LAURA: You really want me to tell you the truth?
16 KATHY: Laura, you're my best friend. I trust your opinion.
17 LAURA: Well, honestly ...
18 KATHY: And I can count on your vote, can't I? I mean, this
19   year's competition is going to be tough!
20 LAURA: How many girls are trying out?
21 KATHY: You mean how many girls *and boys* are trying out?
22 LAURA: Oh yeah, because the boys have to catch the girls
23   after they're tossed in the air so they don't land on their
24   head. Kathy, do you actually think you can do those
25   moves? You know, being thrown up in the air while
26   doing a somersault or the splits?

1 KATHY: How about this move after the boys throw me in the
2   air? *(Demonstrates a terrible move.)*
3 LAURA: Wow. I don't know what to say.
4 KATHY: Good, huh?
5 LAURA: Different. That's for sure. So, how many girls are
6   trying out?
7 KATHY: Forty-two.
8 LAURA: *Forty-two?!* Are you serious?
9 KATHY: I'm afraid so. Everyone wants to be a cheerleader!
10 LAURA: Not me.
11 KATHY: All those cute little outfits, being the center of attention,
12   not to mention all the boys that want to date you ...
13 LAURA: If forty-two are trying out, that means, let's see ...
14   that means thirty-two won't make it!
15 KATHY: I know! Isn't that sad? But I think I've got a really
16   good chance. Especially with this move. *(Demonstrates*
17   *another bad move.)* Plus my original cheer! "We are, we
18   are, we are the Tigers! We are, we are, we are the
19   Tigers! Go! Fight! Win!"
20 LAURA: Kathy, I have to be honest with you.
21 KATHY: Sure! Be honest with me! I'm good, aren't I?
22 LAURA: I'm sorry, but you're terrible!
23 KATHY: Terrible?
24 LAURA: I'm sorry, but you are.
25 KATHY: *(Pointing her finger)* You're trying out too, aren't
26   you?
27 LAURA: No!
28 KATHY: And you're trying to discourage me so that you
29   don't have to compete against me, isn't that right?
30 LAURA: No!
31 KATHY: Well, it won't work! Because you cannot talk me out
32   of this! So, we'll just have to let the students decide who
33   is best. And with my moves and my original cheer, well,
34   what can I say? Except, I've already got this competition
35   nailed!

1 LAURA: Kathy, I'm not trying out!

2 KATHY: Oh yeah? Then why are you telling me that I'm

3   terrible?

4 LAURA: *(Looks into her eyes.)* Why do you think?

5 KATHY: Because I'll become all popular when I'm a

6   cheerleader next year. It's called *jealousy*!

7 LAURA: Kathy, believe me, I'm not jealous!

8 KATHY: Then what is it? Tell me!

9 LAURA: I don't want you to embarrass yourself! Look,

10   Kathy, most of the girls trying out have been in

11   gymnastics or dance for years. Can you even do the

12   splits? Or a back handspring? Or any of those difficult

13   moves?

14 KATHY: Probably! Here, I'll try the splits! *(Attempts, but can*

15   *barely go down.)* Ouch! This hurts!

16 LAURA: Cheerleading isn't your thing, Kathy. I'm sorry.

17 KATHY: But I have my original cheer!

18 LAURA: Then maybe you should ask to be the Cheerleading

19   Coach's Assistant. You know, help with ideas, new

20   cheers ...

21 KATHY: But I want to be a cheerleader! I want to wear that

22   cute little outfit and be thrown into the air ... *(Looks up.)*

23   Well, not really that high, but sort of high. I hope they

24   don't drop me ... Do you think they ever drop the girls?

25   Well, it doesn't matter because we'll have all summer to

26   practice. And my original cheer is going to get me the

27   votes! "We are, we are, we are the Tigers! We are, we

28   are, we are the Tigers! Go! Fight! Win!" *(Smiles proudly*

29   *as she finishes.)* Jealous?

30 LAURA: No. Not in the least.

6. Bad Manners

Cast: KRISTIN, MICHELLE
Props: Child's toy, tissue, trash can.
Setting: A classroom.

1 *(AT RISE: KRISTIN and MICHELLE are standing in front of*
2 *the class.)*
3 **KRISTIN:** *(To the audience)* **For our assignment, Michelle and I**
4 **wrote our own skit called, "Bad Manners." It's intended**
5 **for young children. I play the part of the mom.**
6 **MICHELLE: And I'm the child.**
7 **KRISTIN:** *(Looks at MICHELLE.)* **Ready?**
8 **MICHELLE: Ready.**
9 **KRISTIN:** *(Picks up a child's toy.)* **Look, Michelle, I bought a new**
10 **toy for you.**
11 **MICHELLE:** *(Grabs the toy.)* **Oh, boy!**
12 **KRISTIN: And what are we supposed to say?**
13 **MICHELLE:** *(Examining the toy)* **It's not the one I wanted!**
14 **KRISTIN: Aren't we supposed to say "Thank you"?**
15 **MICHELLE: Oh yeah. Thank you, Mommy.** *(Puts finger in nose.)*
16 **KRISTIN: You're welcome, sweetheart. Michelle! Michelle! Stop**
17 **that! Don't put your finger in your nose!**
18 **MICHELLE: But I needed to get it out!**
19 **KRISTIN: Then take a tissue and gently blow your nose.** *(Hands*
20 *her a tissue.)*
21 **MICHELLE:** *(Blows loudly, then looks in tissue.)* **That was a big**
22 **one. Wanna see?**
23 **KRISTIN: No! Now go throw your tissue away.**
24 **MICHELLE: OK.** *(Wads the tissue and throws it on the ground.)*
25 **KRISTIN: Michelle, are we supposed to throw our trash on the**
26 **ground?**

1 **MICHELLE:** I don't know.

2 **KRISTIN:** No we're not. Now, pick up the tissue and take it to

3   the trash can.

4 **MICHELLE:** But it's dirty! I don't want to touch it!

5 **KRISTIN:** No one else wants to touch it either. It's your trash, so

6   you throw it away.

7 **MICHELLE:** Can't we let it blow away?

8 **KRISTIN:** No. That would make you a litterbug. Pick it up and

9   throw it away.

10 **MICHELLE:** *(Carefully picks up the tissue, examining it.)* **Look!**

11   **It's stuck to the tissue!**

12 **KRISTIN:** What's stuck to the tissue?

13 **MICHELLE:** My booger!

14 **KRISTIN:** Michelle, throw it away!

15 **MICHELLE:** Sure you don't want to see it before I put it in the

16   trash?

17 **KRISTIN:** I'm sure.

18 **MICHELLE:** *(Disappointed)* **OK.** *(Throws the tissue away.)*

19 **KRISTIN:** Thank you. Now, what are you supposed to say?

20 **MICHELLE:** I forgot.

21 **KRISTIN:** You know. I say "thank you," and you say ... Come on,

22   you know.

23 **MICHELLE:** No problem?

24 **KRISTIN:** No. You say, "You're welcome."

25 **MICHELLE:** Oh. *(Sneezes.)*

26 **KRISTIN:** And what are we supposed to say when we sneeze?

27 **MICHELLE:** Kazuntite?

28 **KRISTIN:** No. We say, "Excuse me."

29 **MICHELLE:** Why?

30 **KRISTIN:** Because it's nice manners.

31 **MICHELLE:** Excuse me because I spit all over you when I

32   sneezed?

33 **KRISTIN:** No. Just "excuse me" is fine.

34 **MICHELLE:** *(Sneezes again.)* **Excuse me!** Did I spit on you?

35 **KRISTIN:** *(Wiping her arm)* Yes. Next time, cover your mouth

1   when you sneeze.

2   **MICHELLE: OK.** *(Sneezes, covers mouth.)* ***Excuse me!***

3   **KRISTIN: Thank you, Michelle.**

4   **MICHELLE: You're welcome, Mommy.**

5   **KRISTIN:** *(Short pause.)* **And that was it. That was our skit.**

6   **Thank you. Thank you very much.** *(Long pause as they look*

7   *around the room.)*

8   **MICHELLE: No one is clapping.**

9   **KRISTIN:** *(Fakes a smile to the audience.)* **I heard someone clap.**

10   **MICHELLE: That was Paul dropping his book on the floor.**

11   **KRISTIN:** *(Still faking a smile)* **I still think I heard someone clap.**

12   **Thank you. Thank you very much.**

13   **MICHELLE:** *(Staring straight ahead)* **They thought our skit was**

14   **stupid.**

15   **KRISTIN:** *(Smiling at the audience)* **Yes, Michelle and I thought**

16   **it would be a great skit to perform at the elementary**

17   **schools. Say to the kindergarten classes.**

18   **MICHELLE: I bet they think we should be in kindergarten after**

19   **performing that skit!**

20   **KRISTIN:** *(To the audience)* **Because that age is vital for**

21   **teaching manners.**

22   **MICHELLE:** *(Turns to KRISTIN.)* **Like teaching kids to throw**

23   **away their boogers? Kristin, that was embarrassing! I told**

24   **you we should have left that part out!**

25   **KRISTIN: Michelle, five-year-olds are always picking their**

26   **noses!**

27   **MICHELLE: Well, you should've been the one that had to pick**

28   **your nose in front of your peers!**

29   **KRISTIN: It was a skit. You were performing.**

30   **MICHELLE: Oh, and what a performance! Me, picking my nose!**

31   *(Leans over as if to whisper.)* **And in front of Jake of all**

32   **people! I think I could just die right now!**

33   **KRISTIN:** *(Smiling at the audience)* **And kids pick their noses all**

34   **the time, don't they? That's why it's so important they**

35   **learn good manners!**

1   MICHELLE: But why did I have to be the kid? Why did I have to
2   be the one to pick my nose in front of everyone?
3   KRISTIN: Because we couldn't both be kids. Someone had to be
4   the mother.
5   MICHELLE: Why couldn't I have been the mother?
6   KRISTIN: Because you're shorter than me.
7   MICHELLE: No I'm not!
8   KRISTIN: *(Smiling)* And why are you dwelling on this right
9   now?
10 MICHELLE: Because I think you should have to pick your nose
11   in front of everyone!
12 KRISTIN: The skit is over. *(Smiles at the audience.)* And
13   everyone is staring at us.
14 MICHELLE: Exactly! You pick your nose and we'll call it even.
15 KRISTIN: Call it even?
16 MICHELLE: And if you'll recall, you wrote the part about me
17   picking the green thing out of my nose even though I told
18   you I didn't want to do it!
19 KRISTIN: How about if you get over it and we'll cross our
20   fingers we make a good grade on our assignment?
21 MICHELLE: Do it!
22 KRISTIN: I'm not about to pick my nose just so you'll feel better.
23 MICHELLE: You did this on purpose, didn't you?
24 KRISTIN: *(Smiles to audience.)* And we really hope you enjoyed
25   our skit titled "Bad Manners."
26 MICHELLE: You wanted to get me back for that time I stuck
27   toilet paper to the back of your pants, didn't you?
28 KRISTIN: Oh, that was mean and you know it!
29 MICHELLE: So you had me pick my nose in front of all my
30   friends!
31 KRISTIN: It was just a skit! How many times do I have to say it?
32 MICHELLE: That *you* wrote while demanding that I play the
33   part of the five-year-old!
34 KRISTIN: And you did a wonderful job. *(To the audience)* Didn't
35   she do a wonderful job?

1 MICHELLE: No one is clapping! So just admit it! Admit it!
2 KRISTIN: All right, yes! Yes, I wanted to humiliate you and
3   embarrass you like you embarrassed me! And I thought
4   this was the perfect way to get you back! Have you pick
5   your nose in front of everyone! And it was funny! I could
6   hardly keep from laughing!
7 MICHELLE: *(To the audience)* Thank you! Thank you very
8   much!
9 KRISTIN: Why are you saying that? No one's clapping.
10 MICHELLE: No, but they're laughing! Thanks to you! *(Walking*
11   *off)*
12 KRISTIN: Where are you going?
13 MICHELLE: To hide.
14 KRISTIN: *(Smiles at audience.)* Yes, and uh ... Thank you. Thank
15   you for, uh ... For watching us. And that's, uh ... All we have.
16   It's uh ... The end. *(Exits.)*

7. Hollywood Beauties

Cast: KYLIE, PAIGE
Props: 2 hand-held mirrors, 2 tissues.
Setting: A hallway.

1 *(AT RISE: KYLIE and PAIGE are holding mirrors in front of*
2 *their faces. After a moment, they lower the mirrors to reveal*
3 *bright red lips.)*
4 **KYLIE: I think we look good!**
5 **PAIGE: Me too!** *(Looks in mirror.)* **Kissable.**
6 **KYLIE:** *(Looks in mirror.)* **Dramatic.**
7 **PAIGE: Stunning.**
8 **KYLIE: Alluring.**
9 **PAIGE: Bold.**
10 **KYLIE: Daring.**
11 **PAIGE: Dynamic.**
12 **KYLIE: A model.**
13 **PAIGE: A movie star.**
14 **KYLIE: Definitely! You know, in the old days the movie stars**
15 **always wore red lipstick.**
16 **PAIGE: Forget pale glossy lips.**
17 **KYLIE: Out with the old, in with the new!**
18 **PAIGE: Attention-grabbing red!**
19 **KYLIE: Yes. And when we walk into first period, all eyes will be**
20 **on us!**
21 **PAIGE: Adorable, they will say!**
22 **KYLIE: What style!**
23 **PAIGE: What attitude!**
24 **KYLIE: Glamorous!**
25 **PAIGE: Beautiful!**
26 **KYLIE: Gutsy!**

1 PAIGE: *(Puts mirror down.)* Wait a minute, Kylie. You don't
2   think they'll laugh, do you?
3 KYLIE: Laugh? Paige, why would they laugh?
4 PAIGE: *(Glances in mirror.)* You know ... say we look ... you know ...
5 KYLIE: *(Glances in mirror.)* Amazing?
6 PAIGE: Stupid.
7 KYLIE: We don't look stupid! We look amazing! *(Pause as they*
8   *both look in the mirror.)*
9 PAIGE: Different.
10 KYLIE: Unique!
11 PAIGE: Clownish.
12 KYLIE: Eye-catching!
13 PAIGE: Funny.
14 KYLIE: Stylish!
15 PAIGE: Kylie, are you sure?
16 KYLIE: Absolutely! And just you wait! Tomorrow I bet that
17   practically every girl in school will follow our lead.
18 PAIGE: Well, pale and glossy is in.
19 KYLIE: But we say retro is in!
20 PAIGE: Are you sure? You don't think we look, you know ...
21   funny?
22 KYLIE: There's nothing funny about our fabulous new look.
23   Think of Marilyn Monroe, Judy Garland, Betty Davis,
24   Audrey Hepburn ...
25 PAIGE: Kylie, I don't think any of our friends are into those
26   classic stars. They probably don't even know who they are.
27 KYLIE: Well, who cares? Because we're going to waltz into first
28   period and amaze everyone! *(Looks in mirror and makes a*
29   *kiss.)* Beautiful!
30 PAIGE: Maybe. Or they'll laugh.
31 KYLIE: If they laugh, then they have no sense of style. Because
32   we look dazzling! Like movie stars!
33 PAIGE: *(Glances in mirror.)* I guess. But, you know, I really don't
34   like people staring at me.
35 KYLIE: Paige, of course we want everyone to stare! That's the

1   point! You see, glamorous women must deal with the
2   paparazzi and fans.
3   PAIGE: Kylie, I don't think we have to worry about the
4   paparazzi or fans at high school. It's not like we're in
5   Hollywood.
6   KYLIE: We might as well be! *(Looks in mirror.)* Because we *look*
7   like two Hollywood beauties!
8   PAIGE: *(Glances in the mirror.)* I think we kind of look like
9   clowns.
10 KYLIE: Would you stop it! We don't look like clowns! We look
11 glamorous!
12 PAIGE: Exaggerated.
13 KYLIE: Daring!
14 PAIGE: Distracting.
15 KYLIE: Breathtaking!
16 PAIGE: *(Quickly wipes off the lipstick.)* I can't do it! I just can't!
17 KYLIE: What's wrong with you? We look great!
18 PAIGE: Maybe, but I'd rather see how everyone reacts to you
19 first.
20 KYLIE: But I thought we were in this together!
21 PAIGE: We were until I kept looking at myself in the mirror and
22 thinking I saw a clown. Kylie, I'm afraid everyone will
23 laugh at us.
24 KYLIE: Well, you're wrong! You'll see! And it's probably better
25 this way. Otherwise everyone will wonder why you're
26 copying me.
27 PAIGE: Copying you?
28 KYLIE: I'll be the only one to enter first period looking like a
29 movie star! And truthfully, I prefer it that way.
30 PAIGE: OK, well that's good. And Kylie, even if the entire class
31 laughs at you when you walk in with your bright red lips,
32 I'll be there for you. *(Looks at watch.)* Hey, the bell's about
33 to ring. Let's go. *(Exits.)*
34 KYLIE: *(Looks in mirror.)* A classic beauty! That's what I am.
35 *(Puts mirror down and starts to exit, then stops and looks at*

1 *herself again.)* **A movie star! Yes, that's what I look like.**
2 *(Starts off again, then stops and looks in the mirror. After a*
3 *short pause, she takes out a tissue and wipes the lipstick off.)*
4 **Whatever!** *(Exits.)*

8. Schedule Changes

Cast: JORDAN, AUDREY

Props: 2 class schedules.

1   *(AT RISE: JORDAN and AUDREY are comparing their*
2   *schedules.)*
3   JORDAN: Audrey, look at my horrible schedule this year.
4   Geometry. Chemistry. US History. Spanish Three. English.
5   Computer Science. And Choir.
6   AUDREY: Wow. Sounds like Choir is your only easy class.
7   JORDAN: And I didn't even sign up for Choir!
8   AUDREY: Why would they stick you in Choir if you didn't
9   choose it as your elective?
10 JORDAN: I don't know. I asked for that cooking class. I heard
11   they make all these awesome foods and then get to eat
12   them. And the teacher, Mrs. Mathis, is supposed to be the
13   best!
14 AUDREY: I bet that class was too full.
15 JORDAN: Yeah, so now I get to sing. And I can't sing!
16 AUDREY: Jordan, just go to the office and request a schedule
17   change.
18 JORDAN: I already tried. And unfortunately I'm stuck in Choir.
19   Even though I stood there in the office and demonstrated
20   to Mrs. Reid that I couldn't sing. So what's your elective
21   this year?
22 AUDREY: I have four. Band. Office Assistant. Computer
23   Graphics. And Yearbook Staff.
24 JORDAN: Four? How did you end up with four electives?
25 AUDREY: I don't know. Lucky, I guess.
26 JORDAN: This isn't fair!

1   **AUDREY: Not to you, but I'm not complaining!**

2   **JORDAN: I wouldn't either!**

3   **AUDREY: Choir should be easy.**

4   **JORDAN: But I'm telling you I can't sing!**

5   **AUDREY: Oh, you can't be *that* bad.**

6   **JORDAN: Oh, yes I can!**

7   **AUDREY: Let me hear something. Anything.**

8   **JORDAN: OK.** *(Sings off tune.)* **Old MacDonald had a farm, E-I-E-**

9   **I-O. And on his farm he had a cow, E-I-E-I-O. With a 'moo-**

10   **moo' here and a 'moo-moo' there. Here a 'moo,' there a**

11   **'moo,' everywhere a 'moo-moo.' Old MacDonald had a**

12   **farm, E-I-E-I-O!**

13   **AUDREY: Whoa! That's enough! You're right, Jordan, you can't**

14   **sing.**

15   **JORDAN: So what am I going to do?**

16   **AUDREY: Well, just open your mouth and *pretend* that you're**

17   **singing.**

18   **JORDAN: Oh, and that's going to be a really fun class.**

19   **AUDREY: Or maybe, if you work really, really hard, you'll**

20   **become a better singer. It could happen.**

21   **JORDAN: Yeah, and I could try out for American Idol and**

22   **become one of the top twelve finalists! Audrey, it's not**

23   **going to happen!**

24   **AUDREY: You could cry.**

25   **JORDAN: What?**

26   **AUDREY: Go back to the office and cry. Maybe Mrs. Reid will**

27   **feel sorry for you and change your schedule.**

28   **JORDAN: You think it might work?**

29   **AUDREY: Heather did it last year. They stuck her in some auto**

30   **mechanic class and she went to the office and cried until**

31   **they changed her schedule.**

32   **JORDAN: What class did she get?**

33   **AUDREY: That cooking class. Surprisingly, they decided they**

34   **could squeeze one more person into that class.**

35   **JORDAN: Then that's what I'm going to do!**

1 AUDREY: But you might want to practice first. You know, make
2   it sound sincere.

3 JORDAN: Good idea.

4 AUDREY: Pretend I'm Mrs. Reid because she's the one who
5   makes all the schedule changes.

6 JORDAN: OK. *(Pretending to cry)* "Oh, Mrs. Reid, can't you
7   change my schedule? They put me in Choir and I can't
8   sing." How was that?

9 AUDREY: *(Shakes head.)* You've got to do better than that.

10 JORDAN: *(Takes a deep breath and tries again.)* "Oh, Mrs. Reid,
11   can you please, *please* change my schedule? They put me
12   in Choir and I can't sing! Really, I can't sing!" How was
13   that?

14 AUDREY: *(Shakes head.)* I think you're going to have to do better
15   than that. Act more devastated. As if your life will come to
16   an end if you are forced to take Choir.

17 JORDAN: *(Cries loudly.)* **Oh, Mrs. Reid! Please, please, please ...**
18   *(Pause as she sobs.)* **Please, I'm begging you ...** *(Drops to her*
19   *knees.)* **Begging you from the bottom of my heart! Please,**
20   **oh, please ...** *(Grabs AUDREY's arm.)* **Please, please, please,**
21   **please, please ... Please get me out of Choir!** *(Cries loudly.)*
22   **I can't sing!** *(Buries head in AUDREY's hand.)* **I can't, I can't,**
23   **I can't!** *(After a pause, looks up.)* How was that?

24 AUDREY: Not bad. Not bad at all. In fact, I'd say you have an
25   excellent chance of getting into that cooking class.

26 JORDAN: *(Stands.)* Great! Hey, you want to come to the office
27   and watch me peform?

28 AUDREY: You bet. This will be fun. But you know ...

29 JORDAN: What?

30 AUDREY: Instead of putting you in the cooking class, they
31   might put you in Drama!

9. Physical Education

Cast: JULIE, KAREN
Props: Backpack, M&Ms.
Setting: Gym.

1   *(AT RISE: JULIE and KAREN are on the floor doing sit-ups.)*
2   JULIE and KAREN: ... ninety-six, ninety-seven, ninety-eight,
3   ninety-nine, one hundred!
4   JULIE: Oh my gosh! We are going to be so sore tomorrow!
5   KAREN: I'm already sore! Coach Lewis is so tough! Push-ups,
6   sit-ups, stretching, running ... You'd think we were
7   training for the Olympics!
8   JULIE: *(Collapses.)* I'm dead.
9   KAREN: I think I lost ten pounds today.
10   JULIE: Thank goodness P.E. is our last class of the day.
11   KAREN: Why?
12   JULIE: Because we stink!
13   KAREN: *(Smells underarm.)* Yep, I stink. I'm going straight
14   home to take a shower.
15   JULIE: I'm going home to take a two-hour nap!
16   KAREN: I hate this class! I hate running and stretching and
17   doing these stupid sit-ups!
18   JULIE: I wish it wasn't required to take stupid P.E.
19   KAREN: I know! And tell me, how does exercise help up
20   prepare us for college?
21   JULIE: It doesn't.
22   KAREN: Then it's not fair! We shouldn't be forced to exercise.
23   JULIE: I agree, but what can we do about it?
24   KAREN: Go to the school board?
25   JULIE: Uh, Karen, you go right ahead. That's too political for
26   me. I'd rather jog around the track. Even though I don't

1   like that either.

2   KAREN: *(Smiling)* Or we could have an injury so we could be

3   excused from P.E. class.

4   JULIE: Like a sprained muscle?

5   KAREN: Except it doesn't take a sprained muscle very long to

6   heal. Not like a broken leg.

7   JULIE: Sounds tempting. But I'd rather go a little smaller, like a

8   broken toe.

9   KAREN: Coach would probably still make us do floor exercises

10   even with a broken toe.

11   JULIE: That's true.

12   KAREN: Or ... if we had asthma ... *(Demonstrates.)*

13   JULIE: Sounds like a good excuse, but you'd have to go to the

14   doctor before Coach would believe that.

15   KAREN: Yep. So much for getting out of this stupid class.

16   JULIE: Yeah, we're forced to exercise and get into shape!

17   KAREN: You know, I'd like to see our parents be forced to get

18   into shape at work! Go through what we have to go

19   through.

20   JULIE: Yeah! Like the last hour of their workday, slip off the

21   high heels and run around the office!

22   KAREN: Drop to the floor and give me fifty!

23   JULIE: Make it a hundred!

24   KAREN: My mom would cry.

25   JULIE: My mom would quit her job.

26   KAREN: Wish we could quit.

27   JULIE: Me too. You know, when I have kids, I think I'll

28   homeschool them so they don't have to take P.E. I'll let

29   them watch T.V. instead.

30   KAREN: And have snacks!

31   JULIE: No jogging around the track.

32   KAREN: No stretching till it burns.

33   JULIE: No sit-ups till you die.

34   KAREN: Or waking up with sore muscles. It'll be T.V. and

35   potato chips for my kids!

1   JULIE: Yeah, but ... What if they get fat?

2   KAREN: I won't let them. I'll just take their food away!

3   JULIE: What if they sneak candy? I do.

4   KAREN: Me too.

5   JULIE: Speaking of ... I have some M&Ms in my backpack. Want

6   some?

7   KAREN: You bet!

8   JULIE: *(Takes candy from her backpack and shares.)* Here you go.

9   KAREN: Thanks!

10 JULIE: *(With her mouth full.)* At least we don't have to worry

11   about getting fat.

12 KAREN: Yeah, thanks to Coach for forcing us to exercise! Hey,

13   these are good! Can I have some more?

14 JULIE: You bet!

10. Bad Weather Day

Cast: BECKY, JENNY
Props: Coats, scarves, gloves, backpacks.
Setting: Outside the school building.

1   *(AT RISE: BECKY and JENNY, all bundled up, are shivering*
2   *and jumping around to stay warm. They are standing in*
3   *front of a door.)*
4   **BECKY: Oh my gosh! It's like ten below out here and they didn't**
5   **even call off school! Hello! How about a bad weather day**
6   **here?**
7   **JENNY:** *(Bangs on door.)* **Open up! We're freezing out here!**
8   **BECKY: Oh, I hate zero hour! It's cold! It's dark! Burrrr! I'm**
9   **freezing!** *(Bangs on door.)* **I think someone forgot to unlock**
10   **the door! Hello!**
11   **JENNY: The only reason I took a zero hour class was because I**
12   **needed the extra credit.**
13   **BECKY: I did it so I could get off early in the afternoons and get**
14   **to my job at the bowling alley.** *(Jogging in place)* **I am**
15   **freezing!**
16   **JENNY:** *(Begins to jog.)* **I thought they'd cancel school!**
17   **BECKY: Me too! And why not? We have two bad weather days**
18   **scheduled on the school calendar. And it's bad weather!**
19   *(Bangs on the door.)*
20   **JENNY: And if they had cancelled school, we could still be in**
21   **our beds, all comfy and warm ...**
22   **BECKY: Under my electric blanket!**
23   **JENNY: Sleeping till noon ...**
24   **BECKY: Oh, brrrr, it's so cold!**
25   **JENNY: I can't feel my toes!**
26   **BECKY: Me neither. Maybe it's frostbite.**

1 JENNY: Probably! *(Jumping up and down)* **Hurry up and open**
2   **the door! We're freezing out here!**
3 BECKY: Make that frozen out here!
4 JENNY: I see a light on inside the building. So what's taking so
5   long?
6 BECKY: I don't know, but I feel like a popsicle!
7 JENNY: I hate the winter!
8 BECKY: Unless it snows. Then it seems more bearable.
9 JENNY: Well, whoever decided to have school today was stupid!
10 BECKY: Brrrr! Maybe we should huddle up next to each other.
11   It might help.
12 JENNY: Good idea. *(They move in close. Pause.)* It's not helping.
13 BECKY: I wish it were summer.
14 JENNY: I wish we could run into a sauna.
15 BECKY: Or climb into a hot tub.
16 JENNY: Or underneath a million blankets.
17 BECKY: Or be in Hawaii!
18 JENNY: *(Bangs on door.)* Open the door! Open, open, open!
19 BECKY: What's wrong with them? They never start late!
20 JENNY: Unless ...
21 BECKY: Do you suppose?
22 JENNY: It wasn't on the radio.
23 BECKY: Or on the TV. At least I don't think it was.
24 JENNY: What if they *did* cancel school?
25 BECKY: *(Her teeth chattering)* **Because it's, it's ...** *(Struggles to*
26   *look at watch.)* **It's seven ten and they haven't opened the**
27   **doors.**
28 JENNY: They should've unlocked them ten minutes ago.
29 BECKY: *(Peering in the window)* I don't see anyone inside.
30 JENNY: What if they did call off school?
31 BECKY: Then we would look pretty stupid standing out here in
32   this freezing weather, banging on the doors, trying to get
33   in.
34 JENNY: And look, there are only two cars in the parking lot.
35   Yours and mine.

1 **BECKY: We are so stupid!**

2 **JENNY: Major stupid!**

3 **BECKY: I'm going home!**

4 **JENNY: Me, too!**

5 **BECKY: Electric blanket, here I come!**

6 **JENNY: Sleeping till noon!**

7 **BECKY: See you tomorrow!**

8 **JENNY: Bye!**

9 **BECKY: Bye!** *(They rush off.)*

11. The Right Place at the Right Time

Cast: AMBER, CLAIRE
Props: Two yearbooks, pens.

1   *(AT RISE: AMBER and CLAIRE are sitting at a table, excitedly*
2   *flipping through their new yearbooks.)*
3   **AMBER: Here, Claire! I want you to sign my yearbook!**
4   **CLAIRE: And I want you to sign mine!**
5   **AMBER: Isn't the cover pretty?**
6   **CLAIRE: I love it!** *(They continue flipping through the books.)*
7   **Oh, look! Here I am at the pep rally! I didn't know they**
8   **took this picture. It's cute, isn't it?**
9   **AMBER: That is cute!**
10 **CLAIRE: And here I am again! Look. That's me and Veronica**
11   **singing our duet at the choir concert.**
12 **AMBER: You look pretty.**
13 **CLAIRE: And here I am with my pants rolled up on crazy sock**
14   **day!**
15 **AMBER: Cute.** *(Becoming less enthusiastic as she flips through*
16   *the yearbook.)*
17 **CLAIRE: Oh, oh, and look at this picture! Me and Matt at the**
18   **Homecoming Dance. Gosh, we look good together, don't**
19   **we?**
20 **AMBER: Like a perfect match.**
21 **CLAIRE: Yeah, I like that picture. Oh, look! Remember this?**
22   **The bonfire! Look, that's me standing in front of the fire**
23   **with all the football players.**
24 **AMBER:** *(Getting a closer look)* **But we went to the bonfire**
25   **together. Where am I?**

1   CLAIRE: Didn't you get stuck behind the band?
2   AMBER: Oh yeah. I could hardly even see the bonfire.
3   Remember how cold it was that night?
4   CLAIRE: I remember that I was really hot standing next to that
5   huge fire.
6   AMBER: Not me. I was frozen stiff.
7   CLAIRE: That was such a fun night!
8   AMBER: I guess.
9   CLAIRE: Oh, oh, look! Here's another picture of me at the
10   bonfire with the cheerleaders. *(Pointing)* That's me. Right
11   there in the middle.
12 AMBER: How did you manage that?
13 CLAIRE: I don't know. I guess I was just at the right place at the
14   right time.
15 AMBER: Cute.
16 CLAIRE: I look popular standing right smack in the middle of
17   the football players, then the cheerleaders.
18 AMBER: Yeah. You look popular to me.
19 CLAIRE: Gosh, as much as they put me in the yearbook this
20   year, you'd think I was class favorite!
21 AMBER: You'd think.
22 CLAIRE: Oh, and here I am with Coach Nichols before the state
23   basketball playoffs.
24 AMBER: How did that happen?
25 CLAIRE: Well, I have Coach Nichols last period, and when they
26   came around to take his picture, he wanted a student to
27   pose with him.
28 AMBER: Lucky you.
29 CLAIRE: Oh, and here I am getting my award for the U.I.L. solo
30   competition.
31 AMBER: Nice.
32 CLAIRE: And remember this? When we tried out for the talent
33   show!
34 AMBER: And there you are. But where I am? I was there. It was
35   a duet, not a solo.

1   **CLAIRE: You were there.** *(Looking closer)* **But I don't see you.**

2   **AMBER: Guess they just zoomed in on you.**

3   **CLAIRE: Well, we both know you were there. I like that picture**

4   **of me with the cowboy hat on. We looked cute, didn't we?**

5   **AMBER: You looked cute. So cute the yearbook committee left**

6   **me out.**

7   **CLAIRE: Oh, don't be silly. They just happened to get me. Too**

8   **bad we didn't win that contest. Oh well. Now, let's look at**

9   **your pictures.**

10   **AMBER: OK.** *(Points.)* **Here I am.**

11   **CLAIRE: Oh, that's just the boring individual class picture.**

12   *(Laughs.)* **You kinda look funny there. Maybe it was your**

13   **hair. I don't know. Or maybe it's the way you're tilting**

14   **your head to the side. That doesn't look very natural.**

15   **AMBER: Thanks.**

16   **CLAIRE: Let me see your other pictures.**

17   **AMBER: I haven't found any other pictures.**

18   **CLAIRE: What?**

19   **AMBER: I haven't found any other pictures.**

20   **CLAIRE: Then you're just not looking hard enough.** *(Pause as*

21   *she looks.)* **I know. Flip to the back of the yearbook and**

22   **find your name. It'll list all the page numbers you're on.**

23   *(They flip to the back. A pause.)* **Oh.**

24   **AMBER: Page one fifty-eight. My class picture.**

25   **CLAIRE: Oh.**

26   **AMBER: My mom paid fifty dollars for this yearbook, and I'm**

27   **only on page one fifty-eight having a bad hair day.**

28   **CLAIRE: Well ...** *(Not sure what to say)* **You have a nice piece of**

29   **memorabilia! And you get to have everyone sign your**

30   **yearbook!**

31   **AMBER: You'll be signing all over mine where your pictures**

32   **are. But what am I going to do when someone asks me to**

33   **sign theirs? Flip to page one fifty-eight and add a**

34   **mustache and horns to my stupid picture?**

35   **CLAIRE: Here, Amber. I want you to be the first one to sign**

1   my yearbook.

2   **AMBER: I want you to sign mine, too.** *(They exchange yearbooks.*

3   *AMBER quickly signs the yearbook.)* **Finished.**

4   **CLAIRE: Uh ... Are you in a hurry? Because if I keep with the**

5   **tradition, I have to leave you a little remark by all of my**

6   **pictures. And this is going to take awhile. In fact, do you**

7   **mind if I take your yearbook to my next class so I can work**

8   **on it?**

9   **AMBER: Sure.** *(They stand to leave.)*

10   **CLAIRE:** *(Holding both yearbooks)* **Next year, just try to do what**

11   **I did.**

12   **AMBER: What's that?**

13   **CLAIRE: Be at the right place at the right time! And smile!**

14   **Always smile!**

12. New Best Friends

Cast: VANESSA, RACHEL
Props: Candy, hall passes, backpacks.
Setting: Counselor's office.

1   (AT RISE: VANESSA is sitting in the office when RACHEL
2   enters.)
3   RACHEL: What are *you* doing here?
4   VANESSA: What are *you* doing here?
5   RACHEL: (Waving a pass) I was summoned to the counselor's
6   office.
7   VANESSA: Me, too. And I was here first so maybe you should
8   leave and come back later.
9   RACHEL: (Sitting down) I'll wait.
10   VANESSA: Why don't you wait outside in the hall?
11   RACHEL: Why don't *you* wait outside in the hall?
12   VANESSA: Because I was here first! You know, maybe they
13   called us both down here for the same reason.
14   RACHEL: And what reason would that be?
15   VANESSA: (Matter of fact) Because we hate each other and can't
16   get along.
17   RACHEL: Well, no counseling session is going to change that.
18   VANESSA: You're right about that.
19   RACHEL: It'd be a complete waste of time.
20   VANESSA: You know what? I bet that Mrs. Warren told Mr.
21   Richards about what happened yesterday.
22   RACHEL: Which was all your fault!
23   VANESSA: Hey, you started it!
24   RACHEL: I was just reacting to what you did!
25   VANESSA: And I was defending myself!
26   RACHEL: Well, you didn't have to throw Milk Duds at me!

1 VANESSA: Maybe I thought you wanted one!

2 RACHEL: In my eye? Oh, sure!

3 VANESSA: You know what? I really can't stand you!

4 RACHEL: Well, that's one thing that we agree on, because I
5   can't stand you, either!

6 VANESSA: And this counseling session is going to be a complete
7   waste of time!

8 RACHEL: Unless ...

9 VANESSA: Unless what?

10 RACHEL: Unless we trick Mr. Richards.

11 VANESSA: How?

12 RACHEL: By making him think that we worked out our
13   differences.

14 VANESSA: You mean, fake getting along with each other?

15 RACHEL: It sure beats one of those long and drawn-out lectures
16   that Mr. Richards is all too famous for.

17 VANESSA: You know what? That's a good idea. Anything to keep
18   from being stuck in this room with you for one more
19   second more than I have to.

20 RACHEL: So, should we practice?

21 VANESSA: What? Practice getting along?

22 RACHEL: At being friends.

23 VANESSA: I guess. *(Fakes a smile.)* Mr. Richards, believe me,
24   Rachel and I have worked everything out.

25 RACHEL: I wouldn't believe you.

26 VANESSA: Well, it's hard to pretend that I like you, OK? *(Takes a*
27   *deep breath.)* OK, let me try this again. *(Fake smile)* Mr.
28   Richards, would you believe it? Rachel and I are no longer
29   enemies!

30 RACHEL: I wouldn't believe it. You're a terrible actress.

31 VANESSA: Fine! Then you try it!

32 RACHEL: OK. *(Fake smile)* Mr. Richards, Vanessa and I have
33   come to the conclusion that our behavior has been
34   unreasonable and immature.

35 VANESSA: *(Laughs.)* You sound like a parent! Talk about not

1   believing someone!

2 RACHEL: Well, it's hard to pretend you like someone that you

3   actually hate!

4 VANESSA: Believe me, I know!

5 RACHEL: Then I guess we'll get to sit in here for an hour, maybe

6   two, and listen to Mr. Richards rant on and on about how

7   we should learn to get along.

8 VANESSA: I'd rather be in Math class!

9 RACHEL: *(Looks at watch.)* And what's taking him so long? I'm

10   hungry!

11 VANESSA: Me too. *(Digs out some candy and eats.)*

12 RACHEL: I mean, I'm starving! *(Watching VANESSA)* **Really,**

13   **really starving!**

14 VANESSA: Here! *(Gives her some candy.)*

15 RACHEL: Thanks.

16 VANESSA: Well, that was a first.

17 RACHEL: First what?

18 VANESSA: First time you ever said thank you to me for

19   anything.

20 RACHEL: Well, that was the first time you gave me candy

21   without throwing it at me!

22 VANESSA: Yeah. Sorry about that.

23 RACHEL: It's OK.

24 VANESSA: Here. You want some more?

25 RACHEL: Thanks.

26 VANESSA: Hey, we're actually getting along.

27 RACHEL: You're right. So maybe it wouldn't be a lie?

28 VANESSA: Let me try this again. *(Deep breath)* Mr. Richards, I

29   don't hate Rachel.

30 RACHEL: You're lying, aren't you?

31 VANESSA: Stop it! I'm trying here!

32 RACHEL: Maybe we should try the truth! Mr. Richards, it's true,

33   Vanessa and I don't particularly care for each other, but I

34   believe we can learn to get along.

35 VANESSA: Yes, if she doesn't talk to me and I don't talk to her!

1 RACHEL: And if she gives me candy every day, I believe I can
2   learn to tolerate her presence.
3 VANESSA: I'm not bringing you candy every day!
4 RACHEL: *(Grabs a piece of candy from her hand.)* It can be a
5   peace offering!
6 VANESSA: Forget it!
7 RACHEL: Then I guess we're not going to get along!
8 VANESSA: I guess not! *(Turn their backs to each other.)* Oh! I hate
9   you!
10 RACHEL: I hate you more!
11 VANESSA: *(Short pause.)* Wait a minute. Why do we hate each
12   other?
13 RACHEL: *(Turns to look at VANESSA.)* Because!
14 VANESSA: Because why?
15 RACHEL: Because … because we're both cute and there's always
16   this competition thing going on between us.
17 VANESSA: And we always seem to like the same guy.
18 RACHEL: And we're always fighting for his attention.
19 VANESSA: And half the time he's not even worth the time and
20   attention.
21 RACHEL: You're right about that.
22 VANESSA: Then maybe we should team up instead of fighting.
23 RACHEL: I never thought about that, but that's a good idea. You
24   know, I really don't have a best friend.
25 VANESSA: Me neither. And the two of us …
26 RACHEL: We could have a blast! *(They share a smile.)* Mr.
27   Richards, we've worked it all out.
28 VANESSA: Really!

13. A New Style

Cast: DARCY, HAILEY
Setting: School hallway.

1   *(AT RISE: HAILEY enters wearing a prom dress.)*

2   DARCY: Hailey, uh ... The prom is months away.

3   HAILEY: I know.

4   DARCY: Then why are you wearing your prom dress? This is

5   just a regular school day, isn't it?

6   HAILEY: Seems fairly regular to me.

7   DARCY: Are you being presented with an award or something?

8   HAILEY: No, I don't think so. But that would be nice, wouldn't

9   it?

10 DARCY: Then why are you wearing your prom dress to school?

11 HAILEY: I felt like it.

12 DARCY: You felt like it? Are you serious?

13 HAILEY: Uh-huh.

14 DARCY: Hailey, aren't you embarrassed?

15 HAILEY: No. Actually, I feel pretty. Do I look pretty?

16 DARCY: Are you seriously going to walk down the halls wearing

17   that?

18 HAILEY: It's not against the dress code to wear a prom dress to

19   school.

20 DARCY: But Hailey, no one wears a prom dress to school!

21 HAILEY: No one, except for me.

22 DARCY: And everyone's going to laugh at you!

23 HAILEY: I don't care. And everyone's going to be looking at me,

24   won't they?

25 DARCY: You can count on that.

26 HAILEY: Good! Then I can show Chris what he's missing!

1   DARCY: By wearing your prom dress to school?

2   HAILEY: By standing out! By looking beautiful! By gracing the

3   halls as if I were a movie star. Because when I wear this

4   dress, I feel like a star!

5   DARCY: You may feel like it, but you look like you're four

6   months too early for the Junior-Senior Prom.

7   HAILEY: And ... I plan to start dressing like this every day.

8   DARCY: Every day?

9   HAILEY: Yes! This weekend I went to the thrift shop and found

10   some used dresses that I can wear. Out with the ragged

11   jeans and in with the glamorous dresses!

12   DARCY: Seriously?

13   HAILEY: Seriously!

14   DARCY: You're going to dress like that every day? Not jeans. Not

15   tennis shoes. But prom dresses?

16   HAILEY: Let's not call them prom dresses; let's call them my

17   everyday attire.

18   DARCY: Hailey, that's a prom dress!

19   HAILY: No, it's just a dress that you associate with the prom

20   because that's the only day most people wear dresses like

21   this.

22   DARCY: True, and there's a reason for that. It's a special

23   occasion. And believe me, school is no special occasion!

24   HAILEY: Well, it's my new style. And Chris will finally notice

25   me as I glide down the halls. *(Demonstrates.)*

26   DARCY: Hailey, he's probably going to laugh.

27   HAILEY: I doubt that. And it will definitely get his attention. In

28   fact, it will get everyone's attention. Everyone will be

29   looking at me! *(Twirls in a circle.)*

30   DARCY: Yeah, they'll be looking at you all right.

31   HAILEY: And be jealous. Jealous that I have the courage to show

32   up to school in something besides jeans and a T-shirt. It's

33   called style. *(Twirls in a circle.)* I should be a model.

34   DARCY: So ... when did you decide to go with this new style?

35   HAILEY: Last Friday night when Chris hung up on me when I

1   asked him to go to the prom with me.

2 DARCY: You asked *him* to the prom?

3 HAILEY: I know it was four months early, but I like to think

4   ahead.

5 DARCY: And he hung up on you?

6 HAILEY: Yes! And ignored all my text messages and e-mails.

7 DARCY: Well, I'd say that was a definite "no."

8 HAILEY: He'll see. I'm not just any ordinary girl. *(Strikes a pose.)*

9   I'm a star! Well, at least I will be one day, so I'm preparing

10   myself and the world for what's about to come!

11 DARCY: Uh-huh ... Then you should get a pair of those big

12   sunglasses to go with your, uh ... new stardom.

13 HAILEY: That's a great idea! And I should probably get my nails

14   done too, don't you think?

15 DARCY: Absolutely! *(Shakes head.)* But it's just too bad ...

16 HAILEY: What?

17 DARCY: It's too bad that your backpack doesn't go with your

18   prom dress.

19 HAILEY: Oh no! I didn't think about that. I should find a

20   glittery one, don't you think? Do you think they make

21   glittery backpacks?

22 DARCY: I don't know.

23 HAILEY: Well, if they don't, I'll just make one. And I just feel so

24   glamorous. Don't I look glamorous?

25 DARCY: Sure. Sure you do. And if you feel good about yourself,

26   then you should wear your prom dress to school every day.

27 HAILEY: Yes, I should. Except, remember, we're not calling it a

28   prom dress. It's just my new style.

29 DARCY: Sure, your new style. And Hailey ...

30 HAILEY: Uh-huh?

31 DARCY: When they laugh at you, you just let them know who

32   you are.

33 HAILEY: *(Strikes a pose.)* A star! At least someday I will be.

34   *(DARCY exits, shaking her head.)*

14. Feature Story

Cast: JADE, LILLY
Props: Legal pad, pen.

1 *(AT RISE: Carrying a legal pad and pen, JADE approaches*
2 *LILLY. If desired, LILLY could be wearing a cheerleading*
3 *outfit.)*
4 **LILLY: So, you're writing a feature story about the cheerleaders**
5 **for the school newspaper?**
6 **JADE: Yes.**
7 **LILLY: Well, ask away! I'll be happy to answer any of your**
8 **questions.**
9 **JADE: OK.** *(Looks at notes.)* **When did you first decide to try out**
10 **for cheerleading?**
11 **LILLY: Oh, that's easy!** *(Proudly)* **When I was three years old!**
12 **JADE: Three years old?**
13 **LILLY: Yes. My mother enrolled me in a preschool cheerleading**
14 **class and from that moment on, I knew that's what I**
15 **wanted to be when I grew up!**
16 **JADE: At three years old?**
17 **LILLY: That's right. I remember it like it was yesterday. Don't**
18 **you remember being three?**
19 **JADE: No.** *(Writing)* **OK, so your dream of being a cheerleader**
20 **started at a very young age.**
21 **LILLY: When I was three!**
22 **JADE: Next question.** *(Looks at notes.)* **What do you like most**
23 **about being a cheerleader?**
24 **LILLY: The boys!**
25 **JADE: The boys?**
26 **LILLY: Yes! All the boys love the cheerleaders!**

1   JADE: Uh ... wouldn't you say that your favorite thing about
2   being a cheerleader is encouraging the fans to have more
3   spirit?
4   LILLY: *(Pause as she considers this for a moment.)* **No. I'd say it**
5   **was the boys. Definitely the boys.**
6   JADE: OK. *(Quickly jots down her answer.)* **Boys. Next question.**
7   **As a cheerleader, you work hard at the games to keep the**
8   **fans excited as they root for their team, so tell me, who's**
9   **been your biggest inspiration?**
10 LILLY: Who's inspired me the most? Wow, that's easy. Me!
11 JADE: You've inspired yourself?
12 LILLY: Oh yes! It's like, when I look in the mirror each
13   morning, I'm inspired to go out there and do my best!
14 JADE: Wouldn't you rather say that the cheerleading sponsor
15   has been a great inspiration? Or perhaps a former
16   cheerleader? Or a coach? Or an enthusiastic fan?
17 LILLY: No. I would just say it was me!
18 JADE: *(Quickly writes.)* **OK. Next question. What are your goals**
19   **beyond high school?**
20 LILLY: Beyond high school? Wow.
21 JADE: When you will no longer be a cheerleader. What are your
22   future plans?
23 LILLY: Wow. Now that's a difficult question. All I've ever
24   wanted to do is be a cheerleader.
25 JADE: But Lilly, you can't be a cheerleader for the rest of your
26   life.
27 LILLY: Are you sure?
28 JADE: I suppose in college ...
29 LILLY: Then, yes! That's what I'll do! I'll be a cheerleader in
30   college!
31 JADE: If you make it.
32 LILLY: I'll make it! Next question.
33 JADE: Then after college? Then what will you do, then?
34 LILLY: After that? Wow, that's another hard question.
35 JADE: You can't be a cheerleader after college.

1   **LILLY: I can't?**

2   **JADE: No.**

3   **LILLY: But maybe I could.** *(Smiles.)* **I could be a Dallas Cowboy**

4   **cheerleader!**

5   **JADE: Lilly, you'd be competing against hundreds and**

6   **hundreds of beautiful and talented girls.**

7   **LILLY: I know. But I'd make it!**

8   **JADE: OK.** *(Writes.)* **College cheerleader. Dallas Cowboy**

9   **Cheerleader. Then what?**

10 **LILLY: Then ... then ... then maybe I'll come back here to this**

11   **silly little town and become the cheerleading sponsor, like**

12   **Ms. Henson.**

13 **JADE: I suppose that's possible. Especially after being a Dallas**

14   **Cowboy Cheerleader.**

15 **LILLY: Except ...**

16 **JADE: Except?**

17 **LILLY: Except I'm going to make sure the girls have the cutest**

18   **outfits ever, no matter the cost! And I think I'll get myself**

19   **a matching outfit and cheer right alongside the girls!**

20   **They'd like that, don't you think?**

21 **JADE: I don't know. Would you like Ms. Henson cheering**

22   **alongside you?**

23 **LILLY: No, but Ms. Henson is old!**

24 **JADE: And you won't be?**

25 **LILLY: No! Well, not for a long, long time!**

26 **JADE:** *(Looking at her notes)* **So, after high school you want to be**

27   **a cheerleader in college, then a Dallas Cowboy**

28   **Cheerleader. Then you want to return to your hometown**

29   **and coach the high school cheerleading squad.**

30 **LILLY: Yeah, that's right. Except you can leave that part out**

31   **about me wearing a matching outfit and cheering**

32   **alongside the girls. I'll have to think about that one.**

33 **JADE: OK.**

34 **LILLY: Any more questions?**

35 **JADE: Well, besides being a cheerleader, do you have any**

1   other goals in life?

2   LILLY: Oh sure! I want to fall in love and marry a millionaire

3   and travel around the world and get discovered and

4   become a famous actress and win an Oscar and... *(JADE*

5   *shakes her head and exits. LILLY follows after her.)* Hey, did

6   you want to ask me any other questions?

15. Streaks, Piercings, and Tattoos

Cast: CHLOE, ERIN

1 CHLOE: My mom is so stupid! She won't let me get streaks in
2   my hair! Doesn't she realize that it's "the thing"?
3 ERIN: Believe me, I understand, Chloe. Because my mom won't
4   let me get my nose pierced! I mean, my gosh, what's the
5   big deal?
6 CHLOE: Sounds fine to me.
7 ERIN: I just want a little diamond stud right here. *(Points to her*
8   *nose.)*
9 CHLOE: And I can't get a tattoo, either! It's not like I want some
10   big biker tattoo. I just want a cute little butterfly on my
11   ankle. Wouldn't that look cute?
12 ERIN: It'd look awesome! I wouldn't mind having a little row of
13   hearts on my ankle. I think that'd be cute.
14 CHLOE: But no! I can't get streaks or a tattoo! At least, as my
15   mother says, "Until I move out!"
16 ERIN: I don't think my mom will let me pierce my nose even
17   after I move out.
18 CHLOE: Erin, she won't be able to stop you then.
19 ERIN: Maybe not stop me, but she'd probably hunt me down
20   and rip it out of my nose! Gosh, she's so old-fashioned!
21 CHLOE: You know, if our moms were teenagers right now,
22   they'd be the biggest losers ever!
23 ERIN: Yeah, probably wear stupid dresses to school.
24 CHLOE: And scarves on their heads so the wind wouldn't mess

1   up their hair.

2   ERIN: *(Laughs.)* I've seen pictures of my mother with those

3   scarves around her hair. And tied under her chin. It looks

4   so stupid!

5   CHLOE: What were they thinking?

6   ERIN: I guess our moms thought they were cute. And maybe for

7   their time, they were.

8   CHLOE: I wonder what the fad will be when our kids are our

9   ages?

10   ERIN: I don't know, but I'm going to let my daughter have all

11   the tattoos she wants! And if she wants her nose pierced,

12   it will be fine with me!

13   CHLOE: And my daughter can put any color in her hair that she

14   wants. Red, blue, pink, yellow, I don't care! I'll even pay for

15   it to be done!

16   ERIN: At least we'll be cool parents.

17   CHLOE: Really. And you know what, when I move out, I'm

18   going to get all those things done. "Like it or not, Mom, it's

19   going to happen!"

20   ERIN: Me too. This nose is getting pierced! *(Laughs.)* Can you

21   imagine our moms with a pierced nose?

22   CHLOE: That'd be cool! They could be like the coolest moms

23   ever!

24   ERIN: And they could tattoo our names on their ankles. I might

25   even consider having Mom tattooed on my butt.

26   CHLOE: Yeah, with a little heart.

27   ERIN: That'd be cute.

28   CHLOE: Man, I really want streaks in my hair!

29   ERIN: And I really want my nose pierced! And a tattoo!

30   CHLOE: I can't wait until I move out and I can do anything I

31   want!

32   ERIN: You and me both. I'm going to be so cute with my

33   diamond stud. Hey, maybe I'll get one on both sides.

34   That'd be different. And maybe a lip ring, too. Do you

35   think I should consider getting one in my eyebrow too?

1   **CHLOE: That'd be cute. And I think I'll get red, white, and blue**
2   **streaks in my hair.**
3   **ERIN: Cute! Wow, Chloe, we're going to look so great!**
4   **CHLOE: I know! Come on, we better get to class.**

16. The Countdown Is On

Cast: NATALIE, STEPHANIE
Props: A calendar.
Setting: A classroom.

1   *(AT RISE: NATALIE and STEPHANIE are sitting at their desks*
2   *in a classroom. They both appear very bored, yawning,*
3   *daydreaming, looking at the ceiling, etc. NATALIE pulls out*
4   *a calendar and counts.)*
5   **NATILIE: Thirty-eight more days until Spring Break.**
6   **STEPHANIE: I can't wait. Remember last Spring Break when it**
7   **snowed?**
8   **NATALIE: A surprise artic blast. That was fun. There was more**
9   **snow that week than there'd been all winter.**
10   **STEPHANIE: Maybe it'll happen again.**
11   **NATALIE: I wish it'd happen tomorrow and they'd cancel**
12   **school.**
13   **STEPHANIE: Me, too. I need a break from these teachers.**
14   **NATALIE: You think they need a break from us, too?**
15   **STEPHANIE: I doubt it. Obviously they like school or they**
16   **wouldn't have become teachers.**
17   **NATALIE: Can you imagine? Going to school your entire life.**
18   **And on purpose!**
19   **STEPHANIE: It's beyond my understanding.**
20   **NATALIE: I wish tomorrow was Saturday instead of Tuesday.**
21   **STEPHANIE: But there is one good thing about tomorrow.**
22   **NATALIE: What?**
23   **STEPHANIE: It'll be *thirty-seven* days until Spring Break.**
24   **NATALIE: The countdown is on!**

1 STEPHANIE: Hey, have you ever pretended to be sick when
2   you're not?
3 NATALIE: You mean fake being sick?
4 STEPHANIE: Have you?
5 NATALIE: No. Have you?
6 STEPHANIE: No. But you know what? Tomorrow would be a
7   great day to have a bad headache and stay home, don't you
8   think?
9 NATALIE: Sleep in and watch TV? Yeah, it sounds great to me. I
10   need a day off.
11 STEPHANIE: I will if you will.
12 NATALIE: And I will if you will.
13 STEPHANIE: Then it's a plan! *(They give each other a high five.)*
14 NATALIE: Except ...
15 STEPHANIE: What?
16 NATALIE: Knowing my mom, she'd probably take me to the
17   doctor.
18 STEPHANIE: Wow. I didn't think about that. My mom might do
19   the same thing. And I hate, I mean, *hate*, going to the
20   doctor.
21 NATALIE: Well, we could lie and say tomorrow is a teachers' In-
22   Service Day.
23 STEPHANIE: Yeah, but that would fall apart when our parents
24   notice that everyone is going to school except for us. My
25   mom works with a couple of parents whose kids go to
26   school here.
27 NATALIE: Well, then ... we could skip.
28 STEPHANIE: And get stuck with Saturday detention? No
29   thanks.
30 NATALIE: Oh! I need a break from school! I need sleep! I need
31   TV! I need a day of rest!
32 STEPHANIE: Me too. But I guess it's not going to happen unless
33   that artic blast hits or we get bold enough to take our
34   chances.
35 NATALIE: Then maybe we should take our chances! Who takes

1   their kid to the doctor for a headache?

2 STEPHANIE: My mom.

3 NATALIE: Or what if we did skip school but we called the office

4   as if we were a parent? *(Changing her voice)* "My daughter,

5   Natalie, won't be in class today because she is feeling ill."

6 STEPHANIE: And if I got caught doing that, my mom would

7   ground me for a month!

8 NATALIE: Yeah, same here.

9 STEPHANIE: This isn't fair! We shouldn't be forced to come to

10   school every day!

11 NATALIE: *(A deep, slow breath)* Thirty-eight more days.

12 STEPHANIE: Unless a blizzard comes.

13 NATALIE: I wish.

14 STEPHANIE: Or we get really, really get sick.

15 NATALIE: It's sad, because that almost sounds like fun.

16 STEPHANIE: Yep. *(Shakes her head.)* Can you imagine *wanting*

17   to be a teacher?

18 NATALIE: Never.

19 STEPHANIE: How many more days did you say?

20 NATALIE: Thirty-eight.

21 STEPHANIE: Yuck.

17. Freshmen

Cast: EMMA, SARA

1   *(AT RISE: EMMA and SARA, seniors, are staring at the*
2   *freshmen students.)*
3   **EMMA:** Those freshmen look like babies this year.
4   **SARA:** Wouldn't you *hate* to be a freshman?
5   **EMMA:** It'd be the worst thing in the world.
6   **SARA:** *(Shaking her head)* Straight out of junior high.
7   **EMMA:** So immature.
8   **SARA:** And always getting lost. *(Imitates.)* Where's the science
9   wing? Oh no! I'm turned around! Which door leads to the
10   gym? Is the lunchroom this way or that way? *(Rolls eyes.)*
11   Please!
12   **EMMA:** They remind me of aliens. Immature little aliens
13   who've invaded *our* school.
14   **SARA:** And they can't even drive! Can you imagine not being
15   able to leave the campus during lunch?
16   **EMMA:** I'd die.
17   **SARA:** Oh, and last week when I walked past the cafeteria
18   during the freshmen lunch hour, it was like romper room
19   in there! Screaming, laughing, running ... do they not
20   realize how stupid they act?
21   **EMMA:** I don't even remember eating in the cafeteria. It was,
22   like, decades ago.
23   **SARA:** We are so past that. And you know what's funny?
24   **EMMA:** Besides freshmen? What?
25   **SARA:** They have this annoying little attitude like they have
26   conquered the world now that they're out of junior high.

1   Isn't that funny?

2   EMMA: I know! They walk around as if they're superior human

3   beings.

4   SARA: If you want to look at a superior human being, just look

5   at a senior!

6   EMMA: Freshmen are geeks.

7   SARA: Talk about being low on the totem pole.

8   EMMA: And a senior would never, I mean, never hang out with

9   a baby freshman.

10   SARA: That would be like sinking to the lowest.

11   EMMA: And have you noticed how short they are this year?

12   SARA: Seems like they get shorter every year.

13   EMMA: Do you remember being in ninth grade?

14   SARA: Those are not my proudest days.

15   EMMA: I had braces, pimples, a dorky haircut, and no sense of

16   fashion. I think my mom was still picking out my clothes.

17   SARA: Well dummy me tried to make friends with a few of the

18   seniors.

19   EMMA: You didn't?!

20   SARA: Big mistake.

21   EMMA: Seniors don't associate with freshmen! Ever!

22   SARA: I had to learn that lesson the hard way.

23   EMMA: It would be like a sixth grader hanging out with a first

24   grader!

25   SARA: I can understand that now, but back then ...

26   EMMA: We were clueless.

27   SARA: I'm so glad we're past all that.

28   EMMA: I know, because there's nothing worse than being a

29   freshman!

18. Hotness

Cast: MARY, ANNA

1 MARY: Anna, if you could pick any boy, and I mean any boy, to
2   ask you to the dance tomorrow, who would it be?
3 ANNA: At this point, I'd pick any boy.
4 MARY: But if you had to choose.
5 ANNA: *Had* to choose? Like I'm the most popular girl in high
6   school and the boys are all lined up?
7 MARY: Come on. Just for fun.
8 ANNA: No, fun would be getting to actually dance at the dance.
9 MARY: At least we get to enjoy the music.
10 ANNA: While we stand there and watch the popular girls dance.
11 MARY: *(Laughs.)* We could dance with each other.
12 ANNA: No way!
13 MARY: I know for a fact that we're not the only ones who don't
14   dance.
15 ANNA: Sure, there's Freddie, J.J., Herman ...
16 MARY: See!
17 ANNA: And why do you think that Freddie, J.J., and Herman are
18   *not* dancing?
19 MARY: Because no one asked them to?
20 ANNA: Because they're geeks, Mary! No one wants to dance
21   with them!
22 MARY: So, what does that say about us?
23 ANNA: Well, I'm not about to call *us* geeks!
24 MARY: That's good. So what would you say? That we're so hot
25   that we scare everyone off?
26 ANNA: *(Smiles.)* I like that.

1 MARY: I'd like it if it were true. Shall we make up some more
2   lies?
3 ANNA: Can you make them sound true?
4 MARY: Sure. I'm hot. You're hot.
5 ANNA: Sounds good to me!
6 MARY: And we're so hot that no one wants to dance with us!
7 ANNA: Yeah!
8 MARY: And our hotness demands space. And that's why all the
9   boys back away from us. Because we don't like to be
10   crowded.
11 ANNA: Yeah!
12 MARY: And when the boys walk past us, it's all they can do to
13   keep from talking to us.
14 ANNA: Yeah!
15 MARY: *(Flips her hair.)* Because we are hot!
16 ANNA: *(Flutters her eyes.)* Hot as they come!
17 MARY: *(Short pause)* Feel better now?
18 ANNA: *(Smiling)* Yes, yes I do!
19 MARY: At least one of us does. Too bad it isn't true.
20 ANNA: So, let's pretend it's true.
21 MARY: Pretend we're not geeks and everyone wants to hang out
22   with us?
23 ANNA: Mary, did you have to put it that way?
24 MARY: Pretend that someone has asked us to the dance?
25 ANNA: Maybe this isn't such a good idea.
26 MARY: Pretend that everyone is not laughing and having fun
27   while we're standing against the wall all bored and lonely?
28 ANNA: Lets focus on the positive.
29 MARY: We could skip the dance.
30 ANNA: We could, but don't you like to go? Just in case ...
31 MARY: Just in case? Just in case a miracle happens? Like the
32   perfect slow song begins to play and Jason McIntire looks
33   across the room and suddenly becomes focused on me ...
34 ANNA: Or me.
35 MARY: Then, as if no one else were in the room, he slowly walks

1   **toward me ...**

2   ANNA: Or me.

3   MARY: *(Demonstrates.)* **Reaching out, asking, "Would you honor**

4   **me with this dance?"**

5   ANNA: And then you come to your senses and realize that it's

6   not Jason McIntire standing there! But it's Herman

7   Sanders, the third!

8   MARY: So it is true! We are geeks!

9   ANNA: Unfortunately.

10   MARY: Then maybe we should do something to change that!

11   ANNA: Like what? Go to the mall and get a makeover?

12   MARY: Yeah! And some new clothes ...

13   ANNA: And maybe a new personality, too?

14   MARY: A new personality?

15   ANNA: To match our new-found hotness.

16   MARY: Yeah, that might work! You think it might work?

17   ANNA: Well, if it doesn't we can stick to my original idea.

18   MARY: What was that?

19   ANNA: Pretend we're hot.

19. A la Naturelle

Cast: MARISSA, BAILEY

1 MARISSA: Bailey, you look different today. Did you cut your
2   hair?
3 BAILEY: No.
4 MARISSA: Change the color?
5 BAILEY: No. My hair's the same. Does it look OK?
6 MARISSA: Yeah, it looks fine, it's just ... something looks
7   different about you today.
8 BAILEY: Oh, that's probably because I skipped the makeup this
9   morning. I decided to go for the natural look.
10 MARISSA: Uh ... but why?
11 BAILEY: Well, my mom is always telling me that I don't need all
12   that makeup. And I think she's right. When I'm thirty or
13   forty years old, sure. But not while I have such young,
14   flawless skin.
15 MARISSA: What? You want to look young? Why?
16 BAILEY: Marissa, I'm showing off my natural beauty! Not
17   covering it up with mounds and mounds of base and
18   powder.
19 MARISSA: No, of course not. That thick makeup is what we did
20   in junior high, before we knew any better.
21 BAILEY: I remember. We looked so ridiculous!
22 MARISSA: Oh, and remember those fake eyelashes we tried?
23 BAILEY: Oh, my gosh! Mine fell off of one eye and I didn't even
24   know it until people were giving me a weird look. And
25   remember that glitter eye shadow we thought was so cool?
26   We looked so stupid!

1 MARISSA: I know. But Bailey, we're in high school now and
2   we've learned the technique to apply our makeup in a
3   more natural way.
4 BAILEY: But why apply it when you can skip it and really be
5   natural?
6 MARISSA: Do you honestly want to look like you're in
7   kindergarten?
8 BAILEY: Marissa, you'd be beautiful without makeup, too!
9 MARISSA: How do you know? You've never seen me without
10   makeup. My little brother says that I look scary when I
11   don't have it on.
12 BAILEY: Oh, he's lying.
13 MARISSA: No, I don't think so.
14 BAILEY: And Marissa, have you noticed how nowadays the
15   models are going for the natural look?
16 MARISSA: Oh, they look natural all right, but it's because they
17   have a makeup artist to make them look that way. There's
18   an art to choosing the right colors and blending and
19   accentuating the positive. Like making their lips look full
20   and kissable.
21 BAILEY: *(Puckering up)* I think my lips look kissable.
22 MARISSA: You need some color. Or some gloss. Or something.
23 BAILEY: So you don't like the *a la naturelle*?
24 MARISSA: Uh, no! It looks babyish. Plus, you look like you just
25   crawled out of bed.
26 BAILEY: I did.
27 MARISSA: That's fine if that's what you want to do, but me ... I
28   spend at least two hours in front of the mirror each
29   morning to make sure I look perfect. A la beautiful!
30 BAILEY: Two hours? It usually took me only thirty minutes. If
31   that long. But today, zero minutes. Zero minutes to the
32   pure, fresh, and wholesome look.
33 MARISSA: You mean the plain look. I'm sorry, Bailey, but I'd be
34   completely embarrassed if I was you.
35 BAILEY: Thanks, Marissa! And you know what? You're starting

1   to make me feel embarrassed!

2   MARISSA: Well, I'm sorry, but I wouldn't be caught dead not

3   wearing my makeup.

4   BAILEY: *(Looks around.)* You have some with you? I left mine at

5   home. Didn't think I'd need it.

6   MARISSA: Yes, but it's in my car. And you know what they say

7   about us going out to our cars between classes.

8   BAILEY: Great! Then maybe this wasn't such a good idea!

9   MARISSA: Then maybe you should go home.

10   BAILEY: I can't just go home because I didn't wear makeup to

11   school and now I realize it was a dumb thing to do!

12   MARISSA: You can if you say you're sick. Go to the office and

13   tell them your stomach hurts. They'll probably believe you

14   since your face looks so pale.

15   BAILEY: I look pale?

16   MARISSA: Pale and ... you know, *blah*.

17   BAILEY: Blah?

18   MARISSA: I'd go home if I were you. Before anyone sees you.

19   BAILEY: You're right! I don't know what I was thinking! This *a*

20   *la naturelle* look is for sick days and sleepovers! Not for

21   school! Not for the boys to see! Not for anyone to see! I'm

22   going home before anyone sees me! *(Hides face and exits.)*

20. Yes or No?

Cast: ERICA, MELANIE
Props: A folded note, a coin, a pen.

1   *(AT RISE: ERICA hands MELANIE a folded note.)*

2   **ERICA: Read this!**

3   **MELANIE:** *(Opens note and reads.)* **"Check yes or no"?**

4   **ERICA: Are we in elementary or what? Couldn't Zach have just**

5   **asked me to my face?**

6   **MELANIE: So ... Which one are you going to check? Yes or no?**

7   **ERICA: Well, I was thinking that I would add a box underneath.**

8   **Maybe!**

9   **MELANIE: Or you could check both boxes. That'd confuse him.**

10 **ERICA: That's true. Yes, I want to break up and no, I want to**

11   **work things out.**

12 **MELANIE: So ... Which is it?**

13 **ERICA: I don't know. What would you do?**

14 **MELANIE: Erica, that has to be your decision. But considering**

15   **the fact that you and Zach have only been going out for a**

16   **month and you're already having problems ...**

17 **ERICA: Then I should check yes.**

18 **MELANIE: But on the other hand, you've had a crush on this**

19   **guy for at least two years and now you've got him.**

20 **ERICA: Then I should check no.**

21 **MELANIE: But if he's going to be the jealous type ...**

22 **ERICA: Then I should check yes.**

23 **MELANIE: Unless it's your fault for making him jealous.**

24 **ERICA: Oh, maybe I should check no.**

25 **MELANIE: But from what I've seen, he's a flirt, too.**

26 **ERICA: Yes!**

1 MELANIE: But so are you.

2 ERICA: No!

3 MELANIE: And he is cute!

4 ERICA: Yes. I mean, no.

5 MELANIE: But who wants her boyfriend flirting with all the
6   girls?

7 ERICA: So yes, I want to break up!

8 MELANIE: Unless it makes you proud that they all want him
9   and they can't have him because he's yours.

10 ERICA: Then no, I don't want to break up.

11 MELANIE: But can you trust him?

12 ERICA: No!

13 MELANIE: Can he trust you?

14 ERICA: Yes! Well, maybe.

15 MELANIE: And then you have to consider that the prom is two
16   weeks away.

17 ERICA: So I should check no.

18 MELANIE: Unless you think it would be a miserable night since
19   all you two ever seem to do is fight.

20 ERICA: Then I should check yes.

21 MELANIE: But it's hard to get a date to the prom at the last
22   minute.

23 ERICA: No.

24 MELANIE: But the decision is yours. You have to do what's in
25   your heart.

26 ERICA: But that's the problem. I'm confused.

27 MELANIE: Well, which way are you leaning?

28 ERICA: I'm in the middle.

29 MELANIE: That's a tough one then.

30 ERICA: So what do I do? Check yes or check no?

31 MELANIE: Well, why don't you give him a note and say, "Do
32   you?"

33 ERICA: But what if he says yes?

34 MELANIE: Erica, he wouldn't have given you a note asking if
35   you wanted to break up if he wanted you to say yes. He'd

1 just have broken up with you.

2 ERICA: Oh. That's true. So that means he doesn't want to break

3 up.

4 MELANIE: That's the way I see it. Do you want to break up?

5 ERICA: *(Looks at the note.)* I'm not sure.

6 MELANIE: Do you want to flip a coin?

7 ERICA: Hey, that's a good idea! *(Takes a coin out of her pocket*

8 *and gives it to MELANIE.)*

9 MELANIE: Heads or tails?

10 ERICA: Heads.

11 MELANIE: OK. Heads you stay together and tails you break up.

12 *(Tosses coin in the air.)*

13 ERICA: What is it? What is it?

14 MELANIE: Check no. You two are staying together.

15 ERICA: *(Takes a pen and checks the box.)* You know, that's what

16 I wanted to do all along. Hey, and would you give this note

17 back to him for me? And later I want you to tell me what

18 he says. What his expression was when he saw my answer.

19 MELANIE: And do you want me to see if he'll meet you at the

20 playground by the swings after lunch?

21 ERICA: Melanie!

22 MELANIE: OK! OK! I'll do it.

23 ERICA: Thanks. And don't forget, I want to hear every little

24 detail.

25 MELANIE: You know, for almost breaking up with this guy, you

26 sure are interested in his reaction.

27 ERICA: I never wanted to break up!

28 MELANIE: But you said you didn't know what you wanted to

29 do. You said you were confused.

30 ERICA: I wasn't confused until he gave me this note. I hadn't

31 even thought about breaking up. But he's the one who

32 brought the subject up.

33 MELANIE: So maybe you should scare him like he scared you.

34 ERICA: And check yes? But I already checked no.

35 MELANIE: Scratch it out.

1   **ERICA: I guess I could. Do you think I should?**

2   **MELANIE: You have to do what's in your heart. But remember,**

3   **he's the one who started this whole breaking up thing.**

4   **ERICA: So maybe he wants to.**

5   **MELANIE: But he's probably just testing you.**

6   **ERICA: I don't want to be tested!**

7   **MELANIE: Then break up with him. Check yes.**

8   **ERICA: But I don't want to break up!**

9   **MELANIE: Then check no.**

10 **ERICA: But ...**

11 **MELANIE: Or ...**

12 **ERICA: Or ...?**

13 **MELANIE: Ignore his note and make him come to you face to**

14   **face. Pretend I'm Zach. "So Erica, I noticed you didn't**

15   **answer my note. So what'll it be? Yes or no?"**

16 **ERICA:** *(Throws her arms around MELANIE and holds on tightly.)*

17   **Oh, Zach, I don't want to break up! I love you!**

18 **MELANIE:** *(Unable to free herself)* **Erica! Erica, let go!**

19 **ERICA: I love you so much! So, so, so, so much!**

20 **MELANIE:** *(Still attempting to break away)* **I'm glad ... and I'll ...**

21   **uh ... give Zach your note.** *(Is finally free.)* **No, you don't**

22   **want to break up! That's a definite no!**

Two Men

21. Parenting

Cast: JOHN, TYLER
Props: 2 baby dolls, backpack.

1   *(AT RISE: JOHN and TYLER enter carrying baby dolls.)*

2   **JOHN:** Tyler, remind me one more time, why did I let you talk

3   me into taking a homemaking class?

4   **TYLER:** Because it was going to be fun.

5   **JOHN:** Yeah, cooking during the first semester was fun, but

6   this? *(Holding out the doll)*

7   **TYLER:** And wasn't it cool when Mrs. Watkins let us create our

8   own egg recipes? Hey, I thought my *Eggs a la Mode* were

9   quite tasty, even though no one else liked them.

10 **JOHN:** Yeah, yeah, the cooking was great, but this ... *(Holds up*

11   *doll.)* This? Parenting?

12 **TYLER:** John, compared to Senior English, this is a cinch. What

13   would you rather do? Study Hamlet or hold a baby?

14 **JOHN:** Neither!

15 **TYLER:** Relax, relax. Carrying around the babies only lasts for

16   a week.

17 **JOHN:** And this is Monday, Tyler!

18 **TYLER:** Yeah, so?

19 **JOHN:** And you think this looks macho? Carrying around a

20   stupid baby doll?

21 **TYLER:** Well, I liked what Mrs. Watkins suggested. So I'm going

22   to see if I can find a baby stroller. That way I can throw my

23   baby and books into it and just push it around.

24 **JOHN:** Are you going to get a diaper bag, too?

25 **TYLER:** Hmmmm ... I didn't think about that. Do you think I

26   should? Or do you think I could just put the baby's diapers

1   and bottles into my backpack?

2   JOHN: Tyler, are you listening to yourself? We're jocks on the

3   football team! We can't go around pushing baby strollers

4   and carrying diaper bags!

5   TYLER: But it's required. If we don't, we'll fail the class.

6   JOHN: Then I'll fail!

7   TYLER: Well, I need the credit, so I'm going to take care of my

8   baby. And Mrs. Watkins said that if we brought back an

9   abused baby who's dirty or appears to be mistreated, it's

10   an automatic zero. *(Looking at the baby and holding it*

11   *gently)* So, I'm going to take good care of little Prince.

12 JOHN: Prince?

13 TYLER: Yeah. I'm going to name him Prince. What are you

14   going to name your baby?

15 JOHN: I'm not going to name my baby anything because I'm not

16   going to carry him around!

17 TYLER: But you don't want to fail homemaking, do you?

18 JOHN: Yes, if it means I have to carry around a dolly!

19 TYLER: Come on, John. It won't be that bad. In fact, it might be

20   fun.

21 JOHN: Fun?

22 TYLER: Yeah. Everyone will be giving us a hard time about it.

23 JOHN: And that's OK with you?

24 TYLER: Sure! And you know, we could ask some of the cute

25   girls in our classes to baby-sit.

26 JOHN: Go for it, Tyler! But I'm not doing this! *(Drops doll.)* I

27   refuse!

28 TYLER: Hey, you dropped your baby!

29 JOHN: So? It's not alive!

30 TYLER: *(Picks it up and dusts it off.)* John, if you turn in an

31   abused doll you get a zero!

32 JOHN: And I don't care! I'm not carrying it around! Hey look!

33   You can have twins!

34 TYLER: Yeah, and maybe I'll get some extra points for caring

35   for your neglected baby. You know, I should probably turn

1   you into Child Protective Services.

2   **JOHN:** Funny, Tyler. But instead, why don't you turn my doll

3   into Mrs. Watkins for me.

4   **TYLER:** Poor thing ...

5   **JOHN:** And hey, if you can get extra points for taking care of

6   mine, too, go for it! I don't care! Because I'm not, I repeat,

7   *not* carrying a baby doll around school for a week! So get

8   your stroller and diaper bag and have fun!

9   **TYLER:** Fine. But will you do me a favor first?

10   **JOHN:** What?

11   **TYLER:** Can you hold the babies while I look for my cell phone?

12   **JOHN:** Hold your babies?

13   **TYLER:** *(Gives JOHN the dolls.)* **Thanks.** *(Digs through his*

14   *backpack.)*

15   **JOHN:** Oh, my gosh! Did you see that?

16   **TYLER:** *(Looking up)* **What?**

17   **JOHN:** Coach Rick just walked by and gave me a weird look.

18   Great! This is just great! I'm a jock holding two baby dolls!

19   **TYLER:** Don't worry about it.

20   **JOHN:** Tyler, come on, man! You can't do this! Let's tell Mrs.

21   Watkins that our babies got abducted and take a zero! We

22   can toss them in the dumpster on our way out!

23   **TYLER:** *(Grabs his doll from JOHN.)* **Hey, I'm not letting anyone**

24   abduct *my* baby!

25   **JOHN:** Tyler, what's wrong with you?

26   **TYLER:** Nothing. I'm just planning on taking good care of

27   Prince. And I suggest you do the same thing to your

28   unnamed baby.

29   **JOHN:** *(Throws doll high in air several times and catches it,*

30   *laughing.)* **My baby would probably come back missing**

31   arms and legs.

32   **TYLER:** Stop it! You're hurting it!

33   **JOHN:** Hurting it? *(Laughs.)* **You really want me to see me hurt**

34   it?

35   **TYLER:** *(Rocking his baby gently)* **Not really.**

1   **JOHN:** *(Suddenly, he pulls off the doll's head.)* **Look! Think I'll get**
2   **a zero now? For turning in a headless baby?**
3   **TYLER: Oh my gosh! You killed it! You killed your baby!**
4   **JOHN:** *(Laughing uncontrollably)* **I'm sorry ... but it's funny! It's**
5   **so funny!** *(Swinging the body and head around)* **Don't you**
6   **think it's funny?** *(TYLER begins to walk off.)* **Hey, where are**
7   **you going?**
8   **TYLER: Home! I want to see if my Mom still has my old baby**
9   **stroller!**
10   **JOHN: Oh, well have fun! Guess I'll go turn my baby into Mrs.**
11   **Watkins.** *(Laughing)* **My headless baby!** *(Tosses head in the*
12   *air.)*
13   **TYLER: Hey John, don't worry. I won't be asking you to baby-sit!**
14   **JOHN:** *(Still laughing)* **Good! I'm glad!**

22. Drama Class

Cast: ANDREW, MR. WATTS
Props: A script.
Setting: A classroom.

1   *(AT RISE: ANDREW enters the classroom. MR. WATTS is*
2   *seated at his desk.)*
3   **ANDREW: Uh, Mr. Watts, you wanted to see me?**
4   **MR. WATTS: Andrew, let me ask you a question. Why did you**
5   **choose drama as your elective?**
6   **ANDREW: Because I'm a good actor.**
7   **MR. WATTS: And why do you think you're a good actor?**
8   **ANDREW: 'Cause I watch a lot of TV.**
9   **MR. WATTS: TV. is not theatre.**
10 **ANDREW: I know. TV. is recorded and theatre is live. But either**
11   **way, I'm just as good as those actors on TV.**
12 **MR. WATTS: And do you enjoy acting?**
13 **ANDREW: Yeah, I love it!**
14 **MR. WATTS: Except during my class, right?**
15 **ANDREW: What do you mean, Mr. Watts?**
16 **MR. WATTS: Well, I have been observing your acting abilities,**
17   **and to be honest ... do you want me to be honest?**
18 **ANDREW: Of course. *(Smiling)* You think I should get an agent,**
19   **don't you? Because I'm way good, right?**
20 **MR. WATTS: No, I wouldn't say that. But what I would say is**
21   **that you seem shy and inhibited.**
22 **ANDREW: No I don't!**
23 **MR. WATTS: Take, for instance, your performance today.**
24 **ANDREW: I thought I did good!**
25 **MR. WATTS: *(Shakes head.)* No, I wouldn't say that.**
26 **ANDREW: Maybe you weren't watching! Here, give me the**

1   **script and I'll do it again!**

2   **MR. WATTS: All right.** *(Hands him the script.)*

3   **ANDREW:** *(Looks at script. Head down. Dryly)* **I can't believe**

4   **she's dead. She was my best friend. My companion. My**

5   **everything. I don't know how I'll go on. Oh, how will I go**

6   **on?** *(Looks at MR. WATTS. Smiles proudly.)* **How was that?**

7   **MR. WATTS: Honestly, it was terrible!**

8   **ANDREW: Terrible?**

9   **MR. WATTS:** *(Takes the script.)* **Here, let me show you real**

10   **acting!** *(Glances at script. Short pause.)* **I can't believe she's**

11   **dead! She was my best friend! My companion! My**

12   **everything! I don't know how I'll go on! Oh, how will I go**

13   **on?** *(Looks at Andrew.)* **Now, do you see the difference?**

14   **ANDREW: I'm sorry, Mr. Watts, and excuse me for saying this,**

15   **but I thought my acting was better than yours. You were**

16   **over-doing it and that just didn't seem realistic.**

17   **MR. WATTS: And you sounded like a dull and non-caring**

18   **human being! Do you think you could've read your lines**

19   **any dryer?**

20   **ANDREW: Hey, everyone has their own acting style!**

21   **MR. WATTS: And you, Andrew, have no acting style! Face it; you**

22   **don't have a dramatic bone in your body.**

23   **ANDREW: That's not true!**

24   **MR. WATTS: I'm sorry, but you'd be better off in another class.**

25   **I think you should change your schedule.**

26   **ANDREW: Change my schedule? Change my schedule?**

27   **MR. WATTS: I'm sorry, Andrew.**

28   **ANDREW: Are you kicking me out of Drama?**

29   **MR. WATTS: I'm sorry.**

30   **ANDREW: No! Please, no!**

31   **MR. WATTS: Look, face the facts. You can't act.**

32   **ANDREW: But that's not true! I can act! I can! And ... and I can**

33   **act and dance at the same time! Did you know that?** *(Does*

34   *a little tap dance.)* **See? And I can sing as well! Put me in**

35   **your next musical!** *(Sings a little tune.)* **See? Dancing,**

1   singing, acting! I can do it all! *(Drops to his knees.)* **Please,**

2   **Mr. Watts, I love this class! Don't kick me out of Drama!**

3   **Please! If you do ... seriously, if you do ... I feel as if I might**

4   **die! And look! My eyes ... my eyes are welling up with tears!**

5   *(Crying)* **I'm begging you! Begging you!**

6 **MR. WATTS: Wow. Now *that* was some good acting! Impressive.**

7 **ANDREW: Really?**

8 **MR. WATTS: Really. If you could act half as well as that when**

9   **you read your script ...**

10 **ANDREW:** *(Stands)* **Oh, but I can! I can!** *(Grabs script.*

11   *Dramatically)* **Oh, my gosh! Oh, my gosh! I can't believe**

12   **she's dead! She was my best friend! Oh, oh, my best**

13   **friend! My companion! My everything! Oh! Oh! Oh!** *(Looks*

14   *at MR. WATTS. A pause.)* **So, can I stay in your Drama class?**

15   *(MR. WATTS nods his head.)***Yes!**

23. Figuring Out Girls

Cast: LUKE, RYAN
Props: A piece of paper.

1   **LUKE: I don't understand girls.**

2   **RYAN: Who does?**

3   **LUKE:** *(Tearing at a piece of paper)* **She loves me, she loves me**

4   **not. She loves me, she loves me not.**

5   **RYAN: Another fight with Darby?**

6   **LUKE: I'll say. She broke up with me.**

7   **RYAN: Again?**

8   **LUKE: I get jealous. She gets mad. So then I act like I don't care**

9   **and she still gets mad. So, what am I supposed to do?**

10   **RYAN: Sounds like you can't do anything right.**

11   **LUKE: I know, but I want her back.**

12   **RYAN: My advice, don't beg.**

13   **LUKE: Oh, she didn't give me a chance to beg. When I ran into**

14   **her after third period, she saw me and gave me one of**

15   **these.** *(Demonstrates, looking away and putting head in the*

16   *air.)*

17   **RYAN: She's trying to punish you.**

18   **LUKE: By pretending that she doesn't know me? I told her I was**

19   **sorry at least a hundred times!**

20   **RYAN: And she loves it. All that groveling. And wouldn't it be**

21   **nice to know what you're sorry for?**

22   **LUKE: Ryan, do you know how many times Darby has told me**

23   **she's sorry about something?**

24   **RYAN: Let me guess. Zero?**

25   **LUKE: Zero!**

1   RYAN: Speaking of your ex-girlfriend, look over there. There
2   she is flirting with Seth.

3   LUKE: Oh, that makes me so mad!

4   RYAN: But if you'll notice, she keeps glancing over here to
5   make sure you're looking. She wants to make you jealous.

6   LUKE: I don't understand this. Why is she doing this?

7   RYAN: More punishment.

8   LUKE: Well, I'm tired of being punished for making her mad!
9   Because no matter what I do, she gets mad at me! I act
10   jealous, she's mad! I act like I don't care, she's mad! I
11   spend every moment with her, she's mad! I give her space,
12   she's mad! It's like her little rules change every day.

13   RYAN: Uh-huh. That's why you can't ever figure out how a girl
14   thinks. But I do have one suggestion.

15   LUKE: What?

16   RYAN: Always do the opposite of what she says. That always
17   throws them off. Makes them insecure and clingy.

18   LUKE: Yeah, I'd like her to feel insecure for a change!

19   RYAN: Like right now, Darby expects you to be hurt by watching
20   her flirt with Seth, right?

21   LUKE: Right.

22   RYAN: But instead, don't even look her way. Turn your back to
23   her.

24   LUKE: Well, that sounds like a good idea! *(He turns.)*

25   RYAN: And to make it even better, start laughing. That'll be the
26   icing on the cake.

27   LUKE: OK. *(He begins to laugh.)*

28   RYAN: She's looking.

29   LUKE: *(Laughing)* This is great! I'll show her! She'll see that I'm
30   not her little puppet who adjusts to her new rules every
31   day! Or every hour! So, if she wants me back, she can just
32   get on her hands and knees and beg! *(Laughs loudly.)* So,
33   what is she doing now?

34   RYAN: I hate to tell you this, but as you were laughing, she
35   practically glared a hole in your back.

1   **LUKE: Good! I showed her!**

2   **RYAN: Yeah, but ...**

3   **LUKE: On her knees, crying and begging, that's what it's going**

4   **to take!**

5   **RYAN: Yeah, but ...**

6   **LUKE: And you know what? I won't take her back immediately.**

7   *(Demonstrates.)* **I'll just cross my arms, shake my head,**

8   **and frown at her as she cries her little eyes out.** *(Laughs.)*

9   **Hey, does it look like she's crying?**

10 **RYAN: Uh ... she left.**

11 **LUKE:** *(Spins around.)* **What? Where did she go?**

12 **RYAN: Well, after glaring a hole through you, she grabbed**

13   **Seth's hand and they walked off together.**

14 **LUKE: What? They were holding hands?**

15 **RYAN: Hey, I thought it was a good idea. I guess it backfired. So**

16   **much for figuring out girls.**

17 **LUKE: Dang!**

18 **RYAN: But I guess you can resort to the ole tried and true.**

19 **LUKE: What's that?**

20 **RYAN: Beg.** *(LUKE nods.)*

24. Hold the Onions

Cast: BRYAN, KYLE
Props: Basketball, cell phone.
Setting: Gym.

1   *(AT RISE: BRYAN is leaning against the wall as KYLE*
2   *periodically bounces a basketball.)*
3   **BRYAN: Hey, Kyle, can I borrow your phone?**
4   **KYLE:** *(Glancing around)* **Uh ... you know we're not supposed to**
5   **bring our phones to school.**
6   **BRYAN: And we're not supposed to chew gum either. Hand it**
7   **over.**
8   **KYLE:** *(Careful not to get caught, he hands the phone to BRYAN.)*
9   **What's so important?**
10   **BRYAN: I need to call Jed and tell him to hold the onions.**
11   **KYLE: What? Hold the onions?**
12   **BRYAN: Yeah.** *(Dialing)* **He's picking up burgers for us to eat**
13   **during History.** *(Listening in the phone)* **He's not**
14   **answering. Oh well. Guess I can scrape them off.** *(Hands*
15   *the phone back.)* **Thanks.**
16   **KYLE: So tell me, how is it you're going to get away with eating**
17   **hamburgers in History class?**
18   **BRYAN: Oh, well, we have a sub for the next few days and Mr.**
19   **Fitzgerald has lined up some movie for us to watch. Like,**
20   ***Mr. Smith goes to the Capital* or something.**
21   **KYLE: That's *Mr. Smith goes to Washington*.**
22   **BRYAN: Oh. Whatever. Anyway, the lights will be off so we're**
23   **going to chow down on some burgers.**
24   **KYLE: Hope you don't get caught.**
25   **BRYAN: Nah. We did the same thing yesterday and the sub**
26   **didn't even have a clue. The only bad thing was that we**

1   had to share our fries with half the students to keep them
2   quiet. Hey, Kyle, can I borrow your phone again?
3 KYLE: I guess. *(Hands him the phone.)*
4 BRYAN: I'm gonna try to call Jed again. Tell him to super-size
5   those fries. Oh, and grab plenty of ketchup. We ran out
6   yesterday. *(Listening into the phone)* Hey, Jed, cut those
7   onions on my burger, OK? And super-size those fries.
8   Yeah, extra ketchup. OK. See you soon. *(Hands the phone*
9   *back.)* Thanks. Perfect timing because he was just about to
10   order.
11 KYLE: And how is it that Jed's not in third period like the two
12   of us?
13 BRYAN: Oh, he skipped. Well, kinda. He's got Band third
14   period, and he told Mr. Carroll that he needed to run an
15   errand. Mr. Carroll doesn't care. He's real easygoing.
16 KYLE: I wish we could've skipped this class today.
17 BRYAN: Yeah, since Coach thought it was too cold to suit out,
18   there's nothing to do. Unless we want to study.
19 KYLE: No thanks.
20 BRYAN: And I'm hungry! Can't wait for that burger and fries.
21 KYLE: You're making me hungry.
22 BRYAN: Then sneak out and drive over to Burger Barn. No one
23   will notice. And I'm sure not going to tell.
24 KYLE: But if Coach finds out, I'm dead.
25 BRYAN: And how's he going to find out? He's in his office
26   talking on the phone. Everyone is scattered all over the
27   place. All you have to do is slip through that door.
28 KYLE: It's tempting.
29 BRYAN: And you know the Burger Barn makes the best burgers
30   in town. Ah ... a double-decker with lots of cheese, piled
31   high with bacon, a few jalapeños ...
32 KYLE: Minus the onions for me, too. Man, you're making my
33   mouth water!
34 BRYAN: Then go for it. I'll cover for you if anything happens.
35 KYLE: You promise?

1   BRYAN: Hey, I'll say you went to the bathroom or something.
2   Besides, how often does Coach take a head count?
3   KYLE: Never.
4   BRYAN: Exactly! Man, you've got to take some chances and have
5   some fun! This is high school! We're supposed to push the
6   boundaries and live it up!
7   KYLE: Uh ... by eating hamburgers?
8   BRYAN: By eating hamburgers during History class! Or eating
9   hamburgers when you're supposed to be in P.E! That's
10   what life is all about!
11   KYLE: I don't know. I've never skipped a class before.
12   BRYAN: Never?
13   KYLE: Never.
14   BRYAN: Man, you've been missing out! So, have you ever
15   chewed gum in class before?
16   KYLE: Of course.
17   BRYAN: But you weren't supposed to! Ever carried your phone
18   to school?
19   KYLE: You know I have. You just borrowed it twice.
20   BRYAN: And you weren't supposed to, were you? See, you're a
21   rebel, just like me!
22   KYLE: You're right! This is high school. And I'm supposed to act
23   crazy and have fun! And besides, I'm hungry!
24   BRYAN: Look, Kyle, I've got your back covered.
25   KYLE: And you know what? I'm going to do it!
26   BRYAN: Go for it, man! Go for it!
27   KYLE: *(As he is walking off)* Double-decker ... no make that a
28   triple. A triple-decker with everything on it. Oh, except the
29   onions.

25. Number Fourteen

Cast: ALEX, STEVE
Props: Two lunch trays, food.
Setting: School cafeteria.

1   *(AT RISE: STEVE is sitting in the cafeteria eating as ALEX*
2   *enters carrying a lunch tray.)*
3   **ALEX: Hey, Steve, can I sit here with you?**
4   **STEVE: Sure, but why aren't you eating lunch with Rachel**
5   **today? You two fighting again?**
6   **ALEX:** *(Sitting)* **You know ... I just don't understand girls.**
7   **STEVE:** *(His mouth full)* **They obviously don't understand me,**
8   **either. They scatter like roaches when I enter a room.**
9   **ALEX: So, last night I didn't call her and now she's not speaking**
10   **to me. Over one stupid phone call!**
11   **STEVE: Why didn't you call her?**
12   **ALEX: I fell asleep!**
13   **STEVE: Did you try telling her that?**
14   **ALEX: Like a hundred times! But she just kept saying, "Don't**
15   **think you can treat me like all those other girls, because**
16   **you can't!" Doesn't it sound like she's overreacting?**
17   **STEVE: Can't really blame her.**
18   **ALEX: Because I fell asleep while studying for a History test?**
19   **STEVE: Because you have a reputation for loving them then**
20   **leaving them.**
21   **ALEX: No I don't.**
22   **STEVE: Hey, us guys don't care about your reputation, good,**
23   **bad, or ugly, but those girls sure do. Because they talk. Not**
24   **to me, but they talk. And believe me, all those girls you've**
25   **dumped this year, how many is it ...?**
26   **ALEX: Thirteen.**

1 STEVE: Well, those thirteen girls hate you now. I'd take just one
2   of them, but, well ... that's just wishful thinking, I guess.
3 ALEX: So my ex-girlfriends hate me?
4 STEVE: Without a doubt.
5 ALEX: So Rachel is feeling insecure about our relationship
6   because of my past?
7 STEVE: She's afraid she'll be number fourteen.
8 ALEX: So how do I convince her she won't be?
9 STEVE: Are you sure you want to ask me? The guy who can't
10   even get one girlfriend?
11 ALEX: Yes. I need some help here, Steve! Rachel's not speaking
12   to me, and I don't know how to get her past her
13   insecurities.
14 STEVE: Well, I'd say that you have to reassure her until she
15   believes you.
16 ALEX: But I'm doing that right now. Every day she asks me if I
17   still love her and if I want to break up. And every single
18   day, I'm saying, "Yes, I still love you, Rachel. And no, I
19   don't want to break up."
20 STEVE: *(Shrugs.)* Maybe she needs more than just your words.
21 ALEX: But what else can I do? Give her flowers?
22 STEVE: No, no, no. That's too old fashioned. So, do you *really*
23   love her?
24 ALEX: I think so.
25 STEVE: Then maybe you should give her a ring.
26 ALEX: *What?* An engagement ring? Are you serious?
27 STEVE: You asked for my opinion.
28 ALEX: But I'm not ready for that! We've only been going out for
29   two weeks!
30 STEVE: Then how about a promise ring? You know, promising
31   her that it will last forever.
32 ALEX: Forever? But that's a long time to promise something.
33 STEVE: As a symbol of your love. Something she could look at
34   every day and be reminded of your commitment to her.
35 ALEX: But ... couldn't I just write her a note instead?

1 STEVE: No! You need to do something special. Something that
2   will prove to Rachel and to the world that you love her.
3 ALEX: Yeah, but I think a promise ring is a little too much at
4   this point in our relationship. Maybe I could save that for
5   our six-month anniversary.
6 STEVE: If you're still dating in six months. That'd be a record
7   for you, wouldn't it?
8 ALEX: Yes, but Rachel is different. I think we might even be
9   dating for the rest of the year. That is, if she doesn't stay
10   mad at me.
11 STEVE: Then do something! Show her how much you care!
12   Show her that she's the only one for you!
13 ALEX: You're right! You're absolutely right! But what?
14 STEVE: *(Shrugs.)* I don't know.
15 ALEX: *(Stands.)* I do! *(Climbs onto the table, waves and screams*
16   *across the room.)* Rachel! Rachel, I love you!
17 STEVE: Alex, what are you doing? You're going to embarrass
18   her! Heck, you're embarrassing me!
19 ALEX: *(Still yelling across the room)* No one, and I mean no one
20   compares to you, Rachel! I love you! Yes, I love you, Rachel
21   McBride! You are my one true love!
22 STEVE: Wow. Do you see how red her face is?
23 ALEX: And I want to tell the world ... well, everyone in the
24   cafeteria ... that I'm in love with Rachel McBride! Yes, you
25   Rachel! I love you! *(Pause as he stares ahead. His smile*
26   *disappears.)*
27 STEVE: Get down!
28 ALEX: *(Gets down. Sadly)* Did you see that?
29 STEVE: Everyone staring and laughing at you? Yes, I saw that.
30 ALEX: Did you see what she did?
31 STEVE: Yep. She left.
32 ALEX: But why would she do that when I was proclaiming my
33   love for her in front of everyone in the cafeteria?
34 STEVE: Because you humiliated her.
35 ALEX: I was trying to impress her.

1   STEVE: Bad idea.

2   ALEX: Now what am I going to do?

3   STEVE: You could go back to my idea about the promise ring.

4   ALEX: But I'm not ready to be engaged or promised or anything

5   like that.

6   STEVE: Then why did you just announce to the whole world,

7   well, the whole cafeteria, that she was your one true love?

8   ALEX: She *is* my one true love! At least for now. Do you think

9   she's going to break up with me?

10   STEVE: *(Shrugs.)* I don't know.

11   ALEX: Then maybe I should break up with her first.

12   STEVE: You're going to break up with her?

13   ALEX: Yeah. I just think it's time to move on.

14   STEVE: So soon?

15   ALEX: Yeah, that's what I'm going to do! I'll pass her a note in

16   English class and tell her that it's not working and that I

17   want to break up.

18   STEVE: But I thought you loved her.

19   ALEX: And I'll say that I hope we can still be friends.

20   STEVE: Good luck with that. So that'll put you up to fourteen.

21   ALEX: Fourteen?

22   STEVE: Fourteen girls who hate your guts. And I can't even get

23   one.

26. Rules

Cast: PAUL, BEN
Setting: A classroom.

1   *(AT RISE: PAUL is sitting at a desk. BEN enters and sits at*
2   *another desk beside him.)*
3   **PAUL: You got detention, too?**
4   **BEN: Yep.**
5   **PAUL: What did you do?**
6   **BEN: Late to class.**
7   **PAUL: How many times?**
8   **BEN:** *(Counting for a minute)* **Fifty-seven.**
9   **PAUL: Wow! That's a lot!**
10   **BEN: Yep. What did you do?**
11   **PAUL: I'm not sure.**
12   **BEN: You don't know?**
13   **PAUL: No. I just walked into class and I was handed this slip of**
14   **paper saying I had to go to jail. I mean detention. Do not**
15   **pass go. Do not collect two-hundred dollars.**
16   **BEN: Your first time here?**
17   **PAUL: Yep. So, I guess you're here a lot, huh? I mean, with fifty-**
18   **seven tardies ...**
19   **BEN: Let's just say that I don't handle rules very well. I believe**
20   **in freedom, and in high school there's not much of that.**
21   **PAUL: True. You know, it doesn't seem fair that adults don't get**
22   **into trouble if they're late for work.**
23   **BEN: Mrs. Stephenson is chronically late to fourth period, and**
24   **she never gets detention.**
25   **PAUL: Doesn't seem fair to me.**
26   **BEN: Yeah, I wonder how adults would like it if they had to be**

1   in their chair at work before a bell rang.

2   PAUL: Or only allowed three bathroom passes.

3   BEN: Or only forty minutes for lunch.

4   PAUL: Or get in trouble for chewing gum.

5   BEN: Or having a snack.

6   PAUL: Or forgetting to turn in an assignment.

7   BEN: But that's what they do to us. Treat us like criminals.

8   PAUL: Rules should be for prisoners. Not high school students.

9   BEN: Yeah, give us more freedom!

10 PAUL: Yeah!

11 BEN: I once wrote an essay on that subject. And my teacher

12   wrote all over it with a red marker, "Rules teach self-

13   discipline." Yeah, whatever.

14 PAUL: Yeah, I think I have plenty of self-discipline.

15 BEN: And I wouldn't be late to class, but I like to go home for

16   lunch and watch TV. And there's this soap I like to watch

17   and I've really gotten into it. Like today, Carrie found out

18   about Josh's affair with Leslie. And the whole time Leslie

19   has been pretending to be Carrie's best friend. And you

20   should have seen her face when she found out the truth!

21   When she started crying ... *(Pause, very emotional. Shakes it*

22   *off.)* I looked up at the clock next to the TV and realized I

23   was going to be late for school! Again.

24 PAUL: Doesn't seem right that you have to sit in this room all

25   because of a TV show. And where's our teacher? The one

26   who's supposed to gripe us out about following the rules

27   then give us a stupid assignment to do?

28 BEN: He's late. But he won't get into trouble for it.

29 PAUL: Well, I think the reason I might be in here was because

30   of plagiarism. I sorta copied my essay. Word for word, off

31   the Internet. It had all these big words in it that I didn't

32   even understand. I think my English teacher knew I

33   couldn't write that good.

34 BEN: That's probably it.

35 PAUL: Or it could've been for wearing my PJ bottoms to class

1   yesterday. I thought it'd look cool.

2   BEN: I don't see a problem with wearing your pajamas to
3   school.

4   PAUL: Or it could've been for opening a can of Coke in the gym
5   last week ... which exploded everywhere.

6   BEN: I bet that was funny!

7   PAUL: It was until I got screamed at and had to clean up the
8   mess.

9   BEN: Hey, you wanna see if we can slip out of here without
10   getting caught?

11   PAUL: What'll happen if we get caught?

12   BEN: Detention. And it's not that bad, is it?

13   PAUL: Yeah, especially when they leave us in here alone. Have
14   you ever snuck out?

15   BEN: I do it all the time. Sometimes it works, sometimes it
16   doesn't. So, you want to?

17   PAUL: Nah. I think I'll just take my punishment and be finished
18   with it. Are you going to?

19   BEN: *(Stands.)* Like I said, I don't handle rules very well. *(Starts*
20   *toward the door.)*

21   VOICE: *(From Off-stage)* **Get back in your chair!**

22   BEN: *(Rushes back to his chair and sits down.)* I guess they
23   caught on to me.

24   PAUL: *(Looks up.)* Yeah, there's a camera pointed right at your
25   desk. They've got your number.

26   BEN: *(Looks at the camera and smiles.)* I really, really don't like
27   rules.

27. Super Glue

Cast: SEAN, CODY

1   *(AT RISE: SEAN and CODY are holding hands and struggling*
2   *to get them apart.)*
3   **SEAN: Can't you get it off?**
4   **CODY: I'm trying!**
5   **SEAN: The Super Glue was supposed to go on our project, not**
6   **us!**
7   **CODY: It wasn't my fault it squirted out all over the place!**
8   **SEAN: Owwww! Quit pulling!**
9   **CODY: I'm trying to get your hand off my hand!**
10   **SEAN: Owwww! That hurts!**
11   **CODY: Tell me about it! OK, let's think. There has to be a way.**
12   *(Pause as they think, then after a moment, they begin*
13   *pulling wildly on their hands again, struggling to get them*
14   *apart.)*
15   **SEAN:** *(They stop to rest.)* **Isn't Super Glue supposed to be**
16   **permanent?**
17   **CODY: That's what scares me. One time my sister Super Glued**
18   **a toy pony to her hair. And mom had to cut her hair off!**
19   **SEAN:** *(Looking at their hands)* **Owwww! Well, we can't go**
20   **around school all day holding hands! And we can't cut**
21   **them off, either!**
22   **CODY: I know that, Sean!**
23   **SEAN: Then do something, Cody!**
24   **CODY: What if it never comes off?**
25   **SEAN: And we have to walk around like this forever?**
26   **CODY: That's a scary concept.**

1   SEAN: And I don't like you enough to be stuck to you all the
2   time.

3   CODY: Ditto, Sean!

4   SEAN: OK, let's think. There has to be something.

5   CODY: Hot water didn't work.

6   SEAN: Ice didn't work.

7   CODY: Think we should go to the emergency room?

8   SEAN: Probably. But if they have to perform surgery, I'm
9   keeping *my* hand!

10   CODY: Well so am I!

11   SEAN: If one has to go, then it can be yours!

12   CODY: We're not cutting off my hand to save yours!

13   SEAN: Then get your hand off of mine!

14   CODY: I'm trying! *(Again, they wildly attempt to pry their hands*
15   *apart.)*

16   SEAN: This isn't working!

17   CODY: I know!

18   SEAN: What do you have next period?

19   CODY: Lunch. Thank goodness.

20   SEAN: I have Algebra. And we're having a test and I *can't* miss
21   it.

22   CODY: Look, Sean, I'm not going to Algebra with you. Especially
23   like this!

24   SEAN: Cody, you may not have a choice. Like I said, I've got to
25   take that test. By the way, are you good in Algebra?

26   CODY: Yes, but I'm not going, do you hear me? Besides, I'm
27   hungry. I was going to grab a burger with Jenny.

28   SEAN: I'm hungry, too, but I've got to take that test!

29   CODY: And you're not coming to lunch with me and Jen!

30   SEAN: Look, obviously we're either going to lunch with Jen or
31   to my Algebra class.

32   CODY: I'm going to lunch!

33   SEAN: And I'm going to Algebra! I've got to take that test! *(Again*
34   *they struggle, attempting to take off in two different*
35   *directions.)*

1 CODY: This isn't working!

2 SEAN: Let go!

3 CODY: I'm trying! Believe me, I'm trying!

4 SEAN: That hurts!

5 CODY: Stop it! *(Finally, they stop.)* Short of surgery, you have any
6   other ideas?

7 SEAN: Hey, you have any fingernail polish remover?

8 CODY: Oh sure! Just let me get over there to my backpack and
9   find it. I'm sure it's next to my pink nail polish! Are you
10   serious? Of course I don't have any fingernail polish
11   remover!

12 SEAN: I bet it'd get Super Glue off.

13 CODY: I bet you're right! So, we need to find a girl, and fast!

14 SEAN: Or we could go to the office. Mrs. Mitchell is always
15   doing her nails. I bet she has some.

16 CODY: Good idea. And if we hurry, we can get unstuck before
17   lunch.

18 SEAN: And before my Algebra class.

19 CODY: Wait. There's just one problem.

20 SEAN: What?

21 CODY: Getting to the office.

22 SEAN: What do you mean?

23 CODY: Think about it, Sean. Are we seriously going to walk
24   down the hall holding hands?

25 SEAN: Oh yeah. I didn't think about that. So what are we going
26   to do? Run?

27 CODY: I guess it's our only choice. Beats strolling down the hall,
28   swinging hands, and smiling.

29 SEAN: Oh man! Let's run really fast!

30 CODY: As fast as possible! *(They run off.)*

28. Most Wanted

Cast: HUNTER, LUCAS
Props: Hat, sunglasses.

1   *(AT RISE: HUNTER enters wearing a hat and sunglasses.)*
2   **LUCAS: Hunter? Is that you?**
3   **HUNTER:** *(Disappointed, he removes the sunglasses.)* **So much**
4   **for my disguise!**
5   **LUCAS: Are you hiding from someone?**
6   **HUNTER: Someone? Yeah, someone! Make that every girl in**
7   **this entire school!**
8   **LUCAS: You're hiding from all the girls? But why?**
9   **HUNTER: Why? Isn't it obvious?**
10   **LUCAS: Uh, not really. Can you clue me in?**
11   **HUNTER: Because, Lucas, I'm the quarterback of our**
12   **magnificent football team. And for the first time since**
13   **1983, we're headed off to the state playoffs. And who's**
14   **leading us to the state playoffs? Me! That's who!** *(Looking*
15   *around, he puts sunglasses back on.)*
16   **LUCAS: And the girls are mad?**
17   **HUNTER:** *(Removes sunglasses.)* **No, you idiot! They all love me!**
18   *(Looks around, puts on sunglasses.)* **And ... they** *all* **want me.**
19   **LUCAS: Really?**
20   **HUNTER: You know that Sadie Hawkins dance they're having**
21   **next weekend?**
22   **LUCAS: Yeah, I'm still hoping someone will invite me. Anyone.**
23   **Well, wait, not anyone. Not Bertha or Josephine. But just**
24   **about anyone else would be OK.**
25   **HUNTER: Well, get this. So far, I've had forty-three girls ask me**
26   **to the Sadie Hawkins Dance.**

1 LUCAS: What? Forty-three?! *(Points to himself, then HUNTER.)*
2   Zero. Forty-three. Man, oh man!
3 HUNTER: And I don't know what I'm going to do!
4 LUCAS: You mean, you don't know who you're going to go with?
5 HUNTER: Sort of. *(Removes sunglasses.)* Look, here's the
6   problem. I've had forty-three girls invite me to the Sadie
7   Hawkins Dance ...
8 LUCAS: Uh ... I'm sorry, but I don't see the problem. But go
9   ahead.
10 HUNTER: Well, obviously I hate to hurt anyone's feelings.
11 LUCAS: Tell me you didn't.
12 HUNTER: I did.
13 LUCAS: You said, "Yes" to all forty-three girls?
14 HUNTER: At the time it seemed like the right thing to do. But
15   now ... Lucas, what am I going to do? Borrow a school bus
16   so I can pick up all my dates?
17 LUCAS: This is bad. Really bad.
18 HUNTER: I know! *(Puts sunglasses back on.)*
19 LUCAS: Why didn't you just tell them that you already had a
20   date? Or that you needed to think about it. Or, "Thanks,
21   but I'm skipping the dance this year." That's it! Don't go!
22   Problem solved.
23 HUNTER: But I have to go! Coach Reid is handing out the
24   trophies for our regional win and he expects the entire
25   team to show up. Followed by a dance in which I have
26   forty-three dates!
27 LUCAS: So far.
28 HUNTER: What do you mean, "so far"?
29 LUCAS: Well, the dance isn't until next week. You still have time
30   to pick up a few more dates. Why, at the rate you're going,
31   you might even get up to sixty or seventy dates. And if that
32   happens, you'll definitely need that school bus. But you
33   know, I don't think the school will let you borrow one. But
34   maybe you could call the bus station and rent a
35   Greyhound for a few hours. I don't know if they do that,

1   but you could always check.

2   HUNTER: Lucas, that's not funny. What am I going to do?

3   LUCAS: Well, for one, you could quit saying, "yes" to all the

4   girls. That would help. Forty-three dates is enough if you

5   ask me.

6   HUNTER: OK, OK, from now on I'll say "no." But that still

7   doesn't solve my problem of having forty-three dates. And

8   no, the Greyhound bus is not an option. Can you imagine

9   all my dates on one bus? Why, they'd probably get into a

10   big fight on the way to the school, then exit the bus with

11   bloody noses, ripped dresses, and ruined hairdos. And all

12   because of me! *(Takes off glasses. Smiles for a moment.)* All

13   because of me.

14   LUCAS: OK, I have an idea.

15   HUNTER: What?

16   LUCAS: Confess.

17   HUNTER: *What?*

18   LUCAS: One by one, tell them you made a mistake and said yes

19   to someone else. Break it to them gently. Very, very gently.

20   HUNTER: Maybe ...

21   LUCAS: But you'll still have one problem.

22   HUNTER: What?

23   LUCAS: Out of those forty-three girls, you have to choose one.

24   HUNTER: Just one?

25   LUCAS: You can give me any of your leftovers. I still don't have

26   a date.

27   HUNTER: But how can I pick just one?

28   LUCAS: Eenie, meenie, miney, moe?

29   HUNTER: Not funny, Lucas.

30   LUCAS: Well, who do you like the best?

31   HUNTER: That's the problem! I like all of them!

32   LUCAS: OK, well which one do you want to give me?

33   HUNTER: You know what? I'm just going to do it!

34   LUCAS: What? Let me have all your dates? No problem! Thanks,

35   Hunter!

1   **HUNTER: I'm going to take my chances and go to the Sadie**
2   **Hawkins Dance with forty-three girls! Because you know**
3   **why?**
4   **LUCAS: Why?**
5   **HUNTER:** *(In a cool manner, puts the sunglasses on.)* **Because I**
6   **can.** *(Struts off.)* **Hey, when you've got it, you've got it.**
7   **LUCAS:** *(Following him)* **But I still need a date! Couldn't you let**
8   **me have one? Come on, Hunter! What are friends for?**

29. Dress Code Violation

Cast: CHRIS, NICK
Setting: Principal's office.

1   *(AT RISE: CHRIS and NICK are sitting in the principal's*
2   *office.)*
3   **CHRIS:** So, why were you sent to the principal's office?
4   **NICK:** Dress code violation.
5   **CHRIS:** Me too.
6   **NICK:** Something about my pants being frayed at the bottom.
7   Please! I can't learn because my pants are a little frayed? I
8   say, big deal!
9   **CHRIS:** Oh, well get this! Somehow missing shoestrings is now
10   a dress code violation.
11   **NICK:** Shoestrings?
12   **CHRIS:** Yep.
13   **NICK:** Stupid.
14   **CHRIS:** Tell me about it.
15   **NICK:** Don't teachers have better things to do than stare at the
16   ground and look for something that no one else will ever
17   notice? Or care about?
18   **CHRIS:** So it's my own unique style to skip the shoestrings. So
19   what? Does that mean I can't learn math or English?
20   **NICK:** And my pants are a little frayed at the bottom because I
21   like to wear them long. Big deal! What do they want me to
22   do? Wear high-waters and look like a dork?
23   **CHRIS:** So, we get to sit here in the office and wait for our
24   mommies to bring us pants and shoestrings.
25   **NICK:** I offered to drive home and change, but no! They

1   wouldn't let me. "Because you can't leave the campus
2   after school starts!"
3   CHRIS: Sounds like we're in prison.
4   NICK: Feels like it.
5   CHIRS: And my mom was furious when I called her at work
6   and told her she needed to go to the store and buy me
7   some shoestrings.
8   NICK: My mom was mad, too.
9   CHRIS: Maybe our moms should team up and tell the school
10   what they think about its stupid policies.
11   NICK: That'd be nice.
12   CHRIS: But it'll probably be me who she gets mad at. "Didn't
13   you read the Code of Conduct?" Uh, like, "No."
14   NICK: Who reads that?
15   CHRIS: The teachers.
16   NICK: Well, I think some of these teachers should be sent home
17   because of *their* dress code violations. Take Mrs. Brown.
18   Have you ever seen the tennis shoes she wears with her
19   dresses?
20   CHRIS: Yeah! That looks worse than my missing shoestrings.
21   NICK: Or my frayed pants. And what about that purple sports
22   jacket that Mr. Johnson always wears?
23   CHRIS: It should be banned.
24   NICK: Or Mrs. Lackey's two-inch fake fingernails? I bet the girls
25   couldn't get away with that.
26   CHRIS: And what about Mr. Jones? All he ever wears is
27   sweatpants. We can't wear sweatpants!
28   NICK: And Ms. Carter was wearing flip-flops last week!
29   CHRIS: Because she broke her toe.
30   NICK: But we can't wear flip-flops! Broken toe or not!
31   CHRIS: I'd like to see the teachers get sent home!
32   NICK: *(Laughs.)* Or have to go to the office and call their spouse
33   for a change of clothes!
34   CHRIS: Yeah, that'd be funny.
35   NICK: You know, we should have a little talk with Mr. Mayes

1   when he shows up.

2   CHRIS: You think?

3   NICK: Yes! We'll shout, "Discrimination!"

4   CHRIS: We will?

5   NICK: Yes! If the teachers can violate the dress code, then so

6   can we!

7   CHRIS: Yeah, but ...

8   NICK: *(Stands.)* Someone needs to speak up! It'd be the same as

9   the teachers telling us not to smoke, then lighting up in

10   class!

11   CHRIS: Well, I don't know if that's a good comparison.

12   NICK: If we can't wear something, then they can't either! And if

13   they can wear it, then we can wear it, too! Sounds fair to

14   me.

15   CHRIS: And you're going to tell our principal that?

16   NICK: As soon as he walks in!

17   CHRIS: *(Moves to another chair.)* Uh ... we never met.

18   NICK: What? You're not in this with me?

19   CHRIS: Nah, but you go ahead. I'll just listen.

20   NICK: But I need the support! Someone to back me up!

21   CHRIS: I'll silently support you. In my mind, I'll be thinking,

22   "That's right! You tell him! Yeah!" Then I'll be praying for

23   you.

24   NICK: What?

25   CHRIS: Praying that you don't get expelled. Wouldn't your

26   mom be surprised when she showed up with your pants,

27   but instead got to take you home?

28   NICK: *(Sits down.)* I'd be dead.

29   CHRIS: Me too. So, I guess we just have to accept it.

30   NICK: Yeah, but I don't have to like it!

30. Mighty Senior

Cast: HENRY, LOGAN
Props: Car keys.

1 HENRY: Hey, Logan! That was a great speech you gave at the
2   student assembly!
3 LOGAN: And you are?
4 HENRY: Me? Oh, I'm Henry John Kirkland, the third.
5 LOGAN: But I don't know you. That's odd. Are you the new
6   foreign exchange student?
7 HENRY: Me? Are you kidding?
8 LOGAN: Then are you a transfer student?
9 HENRY: I guess you could call me a transfer student.
10 LOGAN: From?
11 HENRY: From Travis Junior High!
12 LOGAN: *(Jumps back.)* You're a freshman?
13 HENRY: First year here at this awesome high school! And you
14   know what the best part is?
15 LOGAN: *(Stepping back further)* What?
16 HENRY: No more stupid uniforms. I can dress as I choose. And
17   I get to leave campus during the lunch hour. Junior high
18   was so ... you know ... junior high-ish.
19 LOGAN: And as a new freshman, you need to learn one basic,
20   but very important, rule.
21 HENRY: Oh yeah? What's that?
22 LOGAN: Seniors don't talk to freshmen!
23 HENRY: They don't? But why not?
24 LOGAN: Because you're a freshman, that's why not!
25 HENRY: That's stupid. Just because you're a senior doesn't
26   mean you're any better than me.

1   LOGAN: Oh, but it does.

2   HENRY: How?

3   LOGAN: Who gets to leave pep rallies and assemblies first?

4   Seniors. Who gets the best lunch hour of the day? Seniors.

5   Who has Senior Skip Day? Seniors. Who turns of legal age

6   during high school? Seniors. Who graduates? Seniors. And

7   who do freshman look up to? Seniors!

8   HENRY: So if we're to look up to you, then why can't we speak

9   to you?

10 LOGAN: How many times do we have to go over this?

11 HENRY: OK, I understand that being a senior rocks, but don't

12   you understand that freshmen will someday be seniors,

13   too?

14 LOGAN: Of course. And when you're a mighty senior like I am,

15   then you will understand where I'm coming from.

16 HENRY: I'll think all freshmen are geeks and won't talk to

17   them, either?

18 LOGAN: Absolutely. And believe me, you won't.

19 HENRY: So what are we supposed to do? Bow down in your

20   mighty presence?

21 LOGAN: You don't have to go that far. But do step aside and stay

22   out of our way because we seniors do own the halls, you

23   know.

24 HENRY: Truthfully, we could care less. Because we freshmen

25   are more interested in acting crazy and having fun.

26 LOGAN: Of course you are. It's what we seniors call immature.

27   Screaming, laughing, running down the halls ... You act as

28   though you are still in junior high.

29 HENRY: We're just having fun! A new school, a bigger school,

30   more freedom ...

31 LOGAN: *(Pats his back.)* Yes, and we understand it can be

32   exciting.

33 HENRY: It's like every day when my mom picks me up from

34   school ...

35 LOGAN: And you see, only freshmen have their mommies pick

1   them up from school. Seniors drive.

2   HENRY: I'm going to take Driver's Ed this summer.

3   LOGAN: Well, good for you. And I'm going to be packing up for

4   college while you're learning to drive on the right side of

5   the street. Like I said ... what did you say your name was?

6   HENRY: Henry John Kirkland, the third.

7   LOGAN: Well, Henry, the seniors own this school, you

8   understand?

9   HENRY: Which means I'm not allowed to talk to you or any

10   other mighty seniors?

11   LOGAN: *(Pats him on the back.)* We'd rather you not.

12   HENRY: Fine!

13   LOGAN: Thank you.

14   HENRY: *(Suddenly)* Hey, Marty, wait up! You want to walk over

15   to The Burger Shack during lunch? *(To LOGAN)* Sure will

16   be nice when I can drive. *(Exits)*

17   LOGAN: *(Shakes head and pulls car keys from pocket.)* **Freshmen.**

31. Personality Overhaul

Cast: PETE, JACK

1 PETE: Why is it that we can never get the pretty girls to go out
2   with us?

3 JACK: Beats me.

4 PETE: Yesterday I asked Lauren to go out with me and you
5   know what she said?

6 JACK: No?

7 PETE: *(Nods.)* So what's wrong with us?

8 JACK: Guess we just don't have *the look*.

9 PETE: What do you mean, "*the look*"?

10 JACK: Whatever it is they're looking for.

11 PETE: But what's so different? Jeans, T-shirts, and tennis shoes
12   ... they all look pretty basic to me.

13 JACK: Maybe it's our faces. Girls like that ... you know ... chiseled
14   look. Like those male models. And have you ever noticed
15   how those guys always have a strand of hair falling across
16   their forehead in just the right way? It's supposed to be
17   sexy, I guess. *(They both mess with their hair.)* And those
18   dark tans. And perfect white teeth. Muscles. *(They inspect
19   themselves.)*

20 PETE: Bryan gets all the popular girls, and he's no model.

21 JACK: I don't know, then.

22 PETE: Maybe it's our personalities.

23 JACK: Yeah, great. Maybe that's it.

24 PETE: So maybe we need a major personality overhaul. You
25   know, come across all macho and self-confident.

26 JACK: Hey, I'm confident the girls don't like me. Even the ugly

1   girls don't like me that much.

2   PETE: Then maybe it all comes down to attitude. What if we

3   walked around as if we were God's gift to women?

4   *(Demonstrates as he does a little strut/walk.)* **Like this.**

5   JACK: Hey, that's pretty cool.

6   PETE: Come on. Try it.

7   JACK: *(Attempts to walk in this new cool manner.)* **How's this?**

8   PETE: Too stiff. You need to loosen up.

9   JACK: *(Tries again.)* **And this?**

10 PETE: Now you're too floppy. *(Demonstrates.)* **Like this!**

11 JACK: Maybe I'm just no good at walking around with an

12   attitude.

13 PETE: Because it all starts up here. *(Taps his head.)* **First you**

14   have to believe in yourself. Believe you're God's gift to

15   women.

16 JACK: But I'm not.

17 PETE: Come on! Believe it! You can do it!

18 JACK: I don't know ...

19 PETE: Repeat after me, "You wanna see cool, then look no

20   further."

21 JACK: Look no further?

22 PETE: *(Demonstrates with a walk.)* **Because I'm cool. That's**

23   right. I've got your number, and I'm here to show you

24   what it's all about.

25 JACK: OK, Let me try it again. "You wanna see cool, then look

26   no further!"

27 PETE: Hey, that was good!

28 JACK: Really?

29 PETE: Really! You've got it down now. So, what do you say we

30   strut our stuff into the cafeteria and show everyone who's

31   got it going on?

32 JACK: Works for me.

33 PETE: That's right, we'll show those girls what they've been

34   missing. *(They begin to strut off with an attitude.)*

35 JACK: They'll come a-running.

1   PETE: Begging.

2   JACK: Fighting for our attention.

3   PETE: Because we've got it going on!

4   JACK: That's right!

32. Tardy

Cast: MIKE, DAVE
Props: Tardy passes, pink and blue.
Setting: School office.

1   *(AT RISE: MIKE enters the office and approaches DAVE, a*
2   *student office worker.)*
3   **MIKE:** Hey, I need a pass.
4   **DAVE:** I see. Well, tell me your excuse so I can determine if it's
5   pink for excused or blue for unexcused.
6   **MIKE:** But you're a student. Don't I have to talk to the principal
7   or at least the assistant principal?
8   **DAVE:** As the office assistant, it's my job to run interference for
9   Mr. Carter and Mr. Davis. They are way too busy to address
10   every student who comes in here with a tardy. So, as I said,
11   what's your excuse?
12   **MIKE:** Yeah, whatever. But since you're a student, then you can
13   just hand over one of those pink passes to your fellow
14   classmate.
15   **DAVE:** Not so fast. I need to hear your excuse first.
16   **MIKE:** Why?
17   **DAVE:** Because as the office assistant, it's my responsibility.
18   **MIKE:** OK, fine. I'm late because I was talking to my girlfriend.
19   Actually, fighting with my girlfriend. We had to get a few
20   things settled. It was important.
21   **DAVE:** That's it?
22   **MIKE:** That's it.
23   **DAVE:** Unexcused. *(Holds out a blue pass.)* **Sorry.**
24   **MIKE:** What?
25   **DAVE:** Unexcused! Next!
26   **MIKE:** *(Turns around.)* **There's no one else here.**

1   **DAVE:** *(Still holding out the blue pass)* **Here you go.**

2   **MIKE: You've got to be kidding! We're both students here! We**

3   **have to stick up for each other!**

4   **DAVE: I'm sorry. I'm just doing my job. Next!**

5   **MIKE: But there's no one else here! What's wrong with you?**

6   **DAVE: On the contrary. If I'm caught bending the rules, then I**

7   **don't get to work in here any longer.**

8   **MIKE: So what? Take a different elective. Something more**

9   **interesting. Like a computer class.**

10   **DAVE: Actually, this job is very interesting. Especially knowing**

11   **that the fate of the students' lives is in my hands. And by the**

12   **way, you should know, after three of these blue slips, it's**

13   **after-school detention for a week. And this will be your ...?**

14   **MIKE: Third!**

15   **DAVE: Wow. That's too bad.**

16   **MIKE: No, what's too bad is you not giving me a break!**

17   **DAVE: I'm sorry, but it's not my job to give you a break.**

18   **MIKE: How about as one student to another?**

19   **DAVE: Sorry.**

20   **MIKE: So, I guess you don't have too many friends, huh?**

21   **DAVE: No, not too many.**

22   **MIKE: That's because you're making enemies by handing out**

23   **all those stupid blue slips!**

24   **DAVE: Not my concern.**

25   **MIKE: Where's the sympathy? The compassion?**

26   **DAVE: How do you spell your last name? I forgot to put it on**

27   **your pass.**

28   **MIKE: Rogers! R-O-G-E-R-S! And thanks! Thanks a lot for**

29   **sending me to detention!**

30   **DAVE: I didn't send you to detention. You did it to yourself.**

31   **MIKE: Well, I hope you never need a favor from someone!**

32   **DAVE: No favors needed, thank you.** *(Hands him a pink pass.)*

33   **MIKE: Hey, I thought you said it was going to be unexcused!**

34   **This is a pink pass!**

35   **DAVE: I was joking with you!**

1 **MIKE: Really?**

2 **DAVE: Do you think I actually care if you're tardy? Well, I don't.**

3   **In fact, take a stack of these pink passes if you want. I**

4   **don't care. They may come in handy next time you're**

5   **running late.**

6 **MIKE: Really?**

7 **DAVE: Really. You see, I just get so bored working in this stupid**

8   **office. Sometimes I like to have a little fun and mess**

9   **around with someone who walks in here needing a pass.**

10   **But, the truth is, I give these excuses out right and left.**

11 **MIKE: So, I bet you have a lot of friends.**

12 **DAVE: And I just made one more, right?**

13 **MIKE: Definitely!**

14 **DAVE:** *(Hands him the pass.)* **Here you go. Excused.**

15 **MIKE: Thanks!**

16 **MIKE: My pleasure!**

33. The Prettiest Girl

Cast: JIM BOB, HAROLD
Props: Two sack lunches.
Setting: Cafeteria.

1 *(AT RISE: JIM BOB and HAROLD, two nerds, are sitting at a*
2 *table in the cafeteria with their sack lunches.)*
3 **JIM BOB:** *(Eating, his mouth full)* **Darlene is the prettiest girl**
4 **I've ever seen.**
5 **HAROLD: I guess. If you like girls.**
6 **JIM BOB: Look at her smile. Her dimples. Those cute little**
7 **freckles on her nose.** *(Suddenly, giving her a huge wave)* **Hi,**
8 **Darlene! Hi! How are you?**
9 **HAROLD: Guess she doesn't feel like talking. Did you see her**
10 **roll her eyes at you?**
11 **JIM BOB: No she didn't!**
12 **HAROLD: Jim Bob, I don't think she likes you.**
13 **JIM BOB: Well, Harold, maybe not as a boyfriend, but as a**
14 **friend she likes me.**
15 **HAROLD: How do you know?**
16 **JIM BOB: Because we sit next to each other in Geometry class**
17 **and she's always talking to me.**
18 **HAROLD: About what? What does she say?**
19 **JIM BOB: She's like, "Hey, do you know the answer to this one?**
20 **Or what about that one?" We talk about math solutions.**
21 **And she smiles at me!**
22 **HAROLD: That's 'cause she's stupid in Geometry, Jim Bob.**
23 **JIM BOB: Look! Look at that! Darlene is smiling at me this very**
24 **minute!**
25 **HAROLD: No she's not. She's smiling at Zach Francisco. You**
26 **know Zach Francisco – the big, mean running back from**

1   our football team.

2 JIM BOB: No, she's smiling at me!

3 HAROLD: *(Shaking his head)* At least you've got confidence ...
4   even if it's based on a lie.

5 JIM BOB: Hey, Darlene! You want to come over here and sit
6   with us?

7 HAROLD: Are you a betting man?

8 JIM BOB: I don't think she heard me.

9 HAROLD: No, I think she heard you.

10 JIM BOB: She's looking for a place to sit down. I want to invite
11   her to sit with us!

12 HAROLD: Really, Jim Bob, I think she heard you.

13 JIM BOB: *(Stands and waves.)* Darlene, over here! Darlene!
14   Darlene!

15 HAROLD: Sit down! You're embarrassing me!

16 JIM BOB: But I'm trying to get her attention. *(Continues to*
17   *wave.)*

18 HAROLD: Jim Bob, you're getting everyone's attention! Come
19   on! Sit down!

20 JIM BOB: No! I told you, I want to invite her to have lunch with
21   us! Maybe I can help her with her Geometry when we've
22   finished eating. *(Waving)* Darlene! Darlene!

23 HAROLD: Will you sit down?

24 JIM BOB: I don't get it. I don't know why she can't see me.

25 HAROLD: Jim Bob, she sees you. Believe me.

26 JIM BOB: *Darlene!*

27 HAROLD: Sit down!

28 JIM BOB: Maybe she can't see me because of all the people
29   standing in the lunch line.

30 HAROLD: She saw you, Jim Bob!

31 JIM BOB: *(Stands on his chair.)* Darlene, over here!

32 HAROLD: What are you doing? Get down!

33 JIM BOB: No! I want Darlene to come and eat with us.

34 HAROLD: Maybe she doesn't want to, ever think about that?

35 JIM BOB: Of course she does. If I can just get her to look this

1   way. *Darlene! Hey, Darlene! (To HAROLD)* **See, she's**
2   **looking!** *(A pause. His smile fades. Toward Darlene)* **Oh, no**
3   **problem.** *(Steps off his chair, then sits down.)* **You're right.**
4   **She doesn't want to eat with me.**
5 **HAROLD: Well, at least you can see her in Geometry.**
6 **JIM BOB: Yeah, and maybe when she asks me for the answers,**
7   **I'll tell her what she just told me!** *(Mimics.)* **"Leave me**
8   **alone, you moron!" 'Cept I won't say moron, I'll say**
9   **Darlene. "Leave me alone, Darlene!"**
10 **HAROLD: And she'll be sorry. Probably fail math class, too.**
11 **JIM BOB: You think?**
12 **HAROLD: Probably.**
13 **JIM BOB: Then maybe I should still help her out.**
14 **HAROLD: If she has the guts to ask you for help after what she**
15   **just did to you.**
16 **JIM BOB: Well, gosh, I don't want her thinking I'm mad at her.**
17 **HAROLD: Why not?**
18 **JIM BOB: Because ... because ... because I just don't!**
19 **HAROLD: I'm sure Darlene realizes that you may never speak**
20   **to her again. Which is exactly what she deserves if you ask**
21   **me.**
22 **JIM BOB:** *(Stands.)* **Hey, Darlene! I'm not mad at you! And I'll**
23   **still give you the answers in Geometry!**
24 **HAROLD:** *(Pulls him down.)* **Sit down!**
25 **JIM BOB: Hey, did you see that?**
26 **HAROLD: The little sign she gave you?**
27 **JIM BOB:** *(Smiling)* **She waved at me! Guess everything will be**
28   **OK now. You know, Darlene is the prettiest girl I've ever**
29   **seen.**
30 **HAROLD: And you're the dumbest guy I've ever seen!**

34. Last Day of School

Cast: JOSH, ANDY

1   JOSH: I think it's stupid how all the girls are going around
2   crying because it's the last day of school. Personally, I'm
3   glad. Time to celebrate!
4   ANDY: What a bunch of babies! "Boo-hoo!" I say, "Hip, hip
5   hooray!"
6   JOSH: They act as if they'll never see each other again.
7   ANDY: Trading phone numbers like everyone is moving far
8   away.
9   JOSH: Well, some of the seniors will be moving, but big deal.
10   That's life.
11   ANDY: Really. And unfortunately, you and I will be back here
12   next year. Same time, same place.
13   JOSH: Maybe that's something to cry about. *(Imitates crying.)*
14   Boo-hoo! I have to come back to school!
15   ANDY: *(Also imitates crying.)* Every single day. It's torture!
16   JOSH: And I'm so used to seeing you every day and now ... now
17   it's as if we're breaking up! Please, Andy, can I have your
18   phone number so we can call each other every single day?
19   ANDY: *(Laughs.)* Please! You know, I like you, Josh, and you're
20   one of my best friends, but if I don't see you this summer,
21   it's no big deal.
22   JOSH: I know! It's like, "Yeah, catch ya later when school starts
23   back up."
24   ANDY: And just look at those girls crying over there.
25   JOSH: *(Shaking head)* Girls are weird.
26   ANDY: I'll never understand them.

1 JOSH: Not in a million years.

2 ANDY: Hey, there's Cassie. Now, that's one girl I'll miss seeing.

3 JOSH: I know, she's great. I heard she's moving to California.

4 ANDY: What?

5 JOSH: Something about her dad getting transferred.

6 ANDY: I didn't know that. Man, we had a blast in Chemistry this
7   year. Sharing notes, passing notes, sometimes making
8   faces at each other across the room. I was starting to think
9   that our friendship was growing into something a little
10   more.

11 JOSH: Kinda like me and Kaci. She's going off to college, so I
12   won't be seeing her anymore. She'll probably have a ton of
13   new guys to hang out with. College guys.

14 ANDY: I hate to say this, but I'm beginning to feel depressed.

15 JOSH: Me too.

16 ANDY: I mean, I can deal with not seeing you until school starts
17   up again ...

18 JOSH: Gee, thanks.

19 ANDY: And even if you moved to Timbuktu over the summer,
20   I'd be like, "Oh well ..." But not seeing Cassie next year ...

21 JOSH: Or Kaci ...

22 ANDY: It hurts. I don't even want to think about it.

23 JOSH: Maybe you should get her phone number and e-mail
24   address.

25 ANDY: *(Tearing up)* I should.

26 JOSH: And I think I'll get Kaci's numbers, too.

27 ANDY: I just can't imagine her not being here next year. No
28   more cutting up in class together, swapping notes, talking
29   about all the people we hate ...

30 JOSH: And so much for me and Kaci. She'll find a much older
31   boyfriend. I don't think she'll wait around for me to
32   graduate from high school.

33 ANDY: I wouldn't count on it.

34 JOSH: I'm really going to miss Kaci! *(Begins to cry.)*

35 ANDY: I'm really going to miss Cassie! *(Begins to cry.)*

1   JOSH: *(Sniffling)* Hey, you got a tissue on you?
2   ANDY: No. But maybe we could ask one of the girls for one.
3   JOSH: Yeah, I saw Megan carrying around a whole box with her.
4   ANDY: Josh, look at us! We're acting like the girls!
5   JOSH: *(Still crying)* I know!
6   ANDY: *(Still crying)* Come on, let's go get all the phone numbers
7   we can.
8   JOSH: Dude, I am going to miss you!
9   ANDY: Me too! *(They stop and hug, then exit.)*

35. Poetry Is Stupid

Cast: AUSTIN, LANDON
Props: Paper, pens.
Setting: A classroom.

1 *(AT RISE: AUSTIN and LANDON are sitting at their desks*
2 *working on an assignment.)*
3 **AUSTIN: This is a stupid assignment. I don't know how to write**
4 **a poem.**
5 **LANDON: You think I do?**
6 **AUSTIN: The only poem I know is *Roses Are Red*. You know**
7 **that one?**
8 **LANDON: Of course I know that one. Who doesn't?**
9 **AUSTIN: Maybe we could use it as a guide. Carnations are pink ...**
10 **LANDON: They can be red, too. Or white. Or probably any color**
11 **for that matter. I think they feed the flowers dye.**
12 **AUSTIN:** *(Writing)* **Carnations are pink ...**
13 **LANDON:** *(Writing)* **Daisies are white and yellow ...**
14 **AUSTIN: Petunias are purple.**
15 **LANDON: Daffodils are ... Hey, what color are daffodils?**
16 **AUSTIN: I don't know. I think they're yellow.**
17 **LANDON:** *(Writing)* **Sounds good to me.**
18 **AUSTIN: OK, so what do we have so far? Mine says, "Carnations**
19 **are pink, petunias are purple ..."**
20 **LANDON: "Daisies are white and yellow, daffodils are yellow ..."**
21 **Mine sounds stupid, doesn't it?**
22 **AUSTIN:** *(Writing)* **Saccharin is sweet ...**
23 **LANDON: Saccharin?**
24 **AUSTIN: I can't use sugar. It has to be different.**
25 **LANDON: Oh. Uh ...** *(Writing)* **Maple sugar is sweet ...**
26 **AUSTIN:** *(Thinking)* **Carnations are pink, petunias are purple,**

1   Saccharin is sweet ... and, and ... and too bad you're not!

2   LANDON: And, and ... and I hate you!

3   AUSTIN: *(Pause as they look at their poems.)* It's not a very good

4   poem.

5   LANDON: Well, it's something. Better than turning in a blank

6   piece of paper.

7   AUSTIN: But if Mrs. Phillips thinks it's terrible, we may still get

8   a zero.

9   LANDON: But this is about the best I can do! I don't know how

10   to write a poem! It's stupid!

11   AUSTIN: Hey, I understand. I'm in the same boat. But our

12   saccharin and maple sugar sounds dumb.

13   LANDON: OK, then how about ... how about ... Pigs are pink ...

14   AUSTIN: Not in real life, just on cartoons.

15   LANDON: Can't they be pink in poems, too?

16   AUSTIN: I guess.

17   LANDON: OK. Pigs are pink, zebras are striped, sardines are

18   gross ... and ... and ... and so are you!

19   AUSTIN: Landon, I'm not sure that's an improvement.

20   LANDON: Well, I'm trying here!

21   AUSTIN: How about something more expressive. Like ...

22   *(Looking around the room)* The glistening of her hair,

23   made me wonder, why didn't she do something, about her

24   dandruff?

25   LANDON: Oh, like that's any better!

26   AUSTIN: I'm trying, too!

27   LANDON: OK, let's try this again. *(Pause as they look around the*

28   *room.)* The room was quiet ...

29   AUSTIN: As students concentrated ...

30   LANDON: Searching and exploring for words ...

31   AUSTIN: Words that would impress ...

32   LANDON: And satisfy ...

33   AUSTIN: And leave one longing ...

34   LANDON: *(After a pause)* For the bell!

35   AUSTIN: For the bell? Boy, you really murdered that poem.

1   LANDON: Thanks. It comes naturally for me.

2   AUSTIN: Oh! I want to finish this stupid assignment! I want it
3   to be over with! *(Again, they glance around the room.)* The
4   clock ...

5   LANDON: Above the blackboard ...

6   AUSTIN: Ticking ...

7   LANDON: Ever so slowly ...

8   AUSTIN: The minutes ...

9   LANDON: Slowly. Ever so slowly ...

10 AUSTIN: As if frozen in time ...

11 LANDON: As if I'm dying ...

12 AUSTIN: Gasping for air ...

13 LANDON: Praying ...

14 AUSTIN: Dying ... *(Suddenly they jump, looking at each other.)*

15 AUSTIN and LANDON: Saved by the bell! *(They gather their*
16   *belongings and stand.)*

17 LANDON: Hey, I just had an idea.

18 AUSTIN: What's that?

19 LANDON: My kid sister is always writing stupid poems. I bet if
20   we paid her ...

21 AUSTIN: Hey, that is a great idea! How about if I come over to
22   your house after school?

23 LANDON: It's a plan.

24 AUSTIN: You think we could pay your sister a little extra to
25   write a poem without all that gushy love stuff?

26 LANDON: Sounds good to me! See ya.

27 AUSTIN: Bye. *(They exit.)*

36. The Invitation

Cast: ZACH, NATHAN
Props: Birthday invitation.

1　*(AT RISE: ZACH approaches NATHAN and hands him an*
2　*invitation.)*
3　**ZACH: Hey, Nathan, you want to come to my birthday party?**
4　**NATHAN: Your birthday party? Are you serious?**
5　**ZACH: That's an invitation right there!**
6　**NATHAN: Your mom still gives you birthday parties?**
7　**ZACH: Every year. So, I hope you can come. There will be cake**
8　　　**and punch and games and ...**
9　**NATHAN: And balloons and hats and party favors?**
10　**ZACH: Of course!**
11　**NATHAN: And are we going to play Pin the Tail on the Donkey?**
12　**ZACH: No. I haven't done that in ...** *(Counts on fingers.)* **Well, in**
13　　　**a couple of years.**
14　**NATHAN: Zach, listen to me. Guys our age don't have birthday**
15　　　**parties with cake and punch. We go do something cool**
16　　　**like hang out with the guys and go skateboarding.**
17　**ZACH: Well, my mom likes to give me a party every year. You**
18　　　**don't have to bring a gift.**
19　**NATHAN: But what's a birthday party without a gift?**
20　**ZACH: Well, you can if you want.**
21　**NATHAN:** *(Opens invitation and reads.)* **Saturday afternoon.**
22　**ZACH: Two p.m.**
23　**NATHAN:** *(Reading)* **"Come for fun and games." Dude, this**
24　　　**makes you sound like you're five years old!**
25　**ZACH: Oh, you know how moms are.**
26　**NATHAN: If my mom were to do this to me, I'd never speak to**

1   her again! Fun and games! Zach, come on!

2   ZACH: But it's always a lot of fun. Last year we took turns being

3   blindfolded and hitting a piñata.

4   NATHAN: Oh boy!

5   ZACH: It was fun!

6   NATHAN: *(Gives him a strange look.)* I bet.

7   ZACH: This year, Mom said something about having a contest

8   with sidewalk chalk.

9   NATHAN: *(Sarcastic)* Wow. What fun.

10 ZACH: The winner gets a prize.

11 NATHAN: What? A sack of candy?

12 ZACH: No.

13 NATHAN: One of those paddles with a ball attached with a

14   string?

15 ZACH: No.

16 NATHAN: A bottle of bubbles?

17 ZACH: No, my mom gives out cool gifts!

18 NATHAN: Like what?

19 ZACH: This year she's giving out new iPods.

20 NATHAN: *What?*

21 ZACH: One for the best sidewalk chalk creation. One for the

22   dart-throwing contest. One for ...

23 NATHAN: Are you serious? She's giving out iPods as prizes?

24 ZACH: Yeah. Last year she was giving out those cool portable

25   DVD players.

26 NATHAN: Awesome!

27 ZACH: And of course there's cake and ice cream. That's my

28   favorite part.

29 NATHAN: Wow! Well, let me just RSVP right now! I'll be there!

30 ZACH: You'll come?

31 NATHAN: Absolutely! An iPod as a prize? Wow!

32 ZACH: And don't forget party favors.

33 NATHAN: Party favors, too?

34 ZACH: Yeah. It's usually gift certificates ... or cash.

35 NATHAN: *Cash?* Wow! *(Pats ZACH on the back.)* I'll definitely be

1   there, Zach! Thanks for the invitation!

2   ZACH: Sure. No problem. Glad you can come. Hey do you want

3   to hear what my theme is this year? Last year it was

4   Batman, but this year I'm going with Spiderman. Mom let

5   me pick it out!

37. Mistaken Infatuation

Cast: JAKE, MATT

1 JAKE: So, did you ask her out?

2 MATT: Unfortunately yes.

3 JAKE: She said no?

4 MATT: She said yes.

5 JAKE: Then why aren't you happy?

6 MATT: Because all year I've looked across the room and
7   thought Jade was the most beautiful girl I've ever seen.
8   She was like a Christmas present. A winning lottery ticket.
9   A watermelon on the first day of summer.

10 JAKE: A watermelon?

11 MATT: And when I thought of her, my stomach would do
12   somersaults. And now ... now ...

13 JAKE: Now? You don't feel the same way now?

14 MATT: Unfortunately, no.

15 JAKE: But I don't understand. What happened?

16 MATT: Did you know that before today I had never actually
17   spoken to Jade?

18 JAKE: But you talked about talking to her every single day. And
19   today you did! So, what's the problem?

20 MATT: The problem is that I thought I liked her.

21 JAKE: And now that you've talked to her you don't?

22 MATT: Exactly.

23 JAKE: But why?

24 MATT: Jake, have you ever talked to her?

25 JAKE: No. I don't even know her. You're the one who's been
26   infatuated with her all year, not me.

1 MATT: And I ask, why? Why have I been so infatuated with her
2   all year?
3 JAKE: Because you thought she was hot.
4 MATT: And from a distance, she is.
5 JAKE: She's not hot up close?
6 MATT: She's OK, I guess.
7 JAKE: Then what's the problem?
8 MATT: Her voice! Oh my gosh! She screeches like this.
9   *(Imitates.)* "Oh, I'd love to go out with you, Matt! I thought
10   you'd never ask!" And now I wish I hadn't asked.
11 JAKE: She screeches like that?
12 MATT: Unfortunately, yes.
13 JAKE: Did you laugh?
14 MATT: No, I didn't laugh! But I kept asking myself, how can I
15   say, "Never mind"? Or, "Sorry, but I take it back"? Or,
16   "Thanks, but no thanks"?
17 JAKE: Well, I guess you could.
18 MATT: Like that would be nice to ask a girl out for a date and
19   then say never mind!
20 JAKE: Well, it's only one date. You can handle that.
21 MATT: I guess. But I'm just so depressed now. How could I have
22   been so taken with Jade for so long, daydreamed about
23   her every single day in class, then in five minutes realize I
24   don't even like her?
25 JAKE: Well, you've learned an important lesson today.
26 MATT: Looks can be deceiving. Wow. I wish I'd never talked to
27   her. Dreaming about talking to her was more fun than
28   actually talking to her.
29 JAKE: Who knows? Maybe you'll like her again after the two of
30   you go out.
31 MATT: If I wear earplugs.
32 JAKE: Maybe she was just excited about going out with you.
33 MATT: Too excited if you ask me. Makes me wonder if she ever
34   gets asked out.
35 JAKE: Maybe she had a sore throat and just sounded funny.

1   MATT: I'm afraid she sounds funny all the time.

2   JAKE: Are you going to kiss her?

3   MATT: *What?*

4   JAKE: That's what you've said all year. *(In a dreamy tone)* "All I

5   want to do is kiss her lips."

6   MATT: I didn't say it like that!

7   JAKE: Yes you did! You said it all the time!

8   MATT: And now I don't even like her! In fact, I despise her!

9   JAKE: All because of her voice?

10 MATT: Man, you should have heard her. *(Imitates her voice and*

11   *jumps up and down to demonstrate her excitement.)* "What

12   are we going to do? When are we going? What time are we

13   going? Can we go today?"

14 JAKE: Sounds like she has more problems than just her voice.

15 MATT: Jake, how am I going to get through this?

16 JAKE: Well, why don't you imagine that she's that girl you

17   always daydreamed about?

18 MATT: It might help, if she doesn't talk.

19 JAKE: Take her to a movie so she has to be quiet.

20 MATT: Good idea.

21 JAKE: Then rush her home and tell her that you have a curfew

22   or a relative just died or something like that.

23 MATT: Yeah, I guess I can do that. But what if she expects me to

24   kiss her goodnight?

25 JAKE: Well, you could close your eyes and pretend it's someone

26   else.

27 MATT: Like the girl I daydreamed about that isn't real?

28 JAKE: Sure. Whatever works.

29 MATT: Man, I wasted a lot of energy thinking about a girl that I

30   don't even like!

31 JAKE: Next time, talk to her first.

32 MATT: Believe me, I will!

38. The Butterfly

Cast: MASON, CALEB

1 MASON: *(Angrily approaches CALEB.)* Hey, Caleb, you better
2   quit talking to my girlfriend!
3 CALEB: What do you mean, "Quit talking to your girlfriend"? I
4   don't have to quit talking to Callie. We're friends.
5 MASON: Look, I don't like her talking to other guys, so I'm
6   warning you.
7 CALEB: Mason, have you ever heard that saying about letting a
8   butterfly go, and if it's yours, it'll come back?
9 MASON: What does that mean?
10 CALEB: If Callie can talk to other guys and still want to go out
11   with you, then you don't have anything to worry about.
12 MASON: But you, Caleb Sawyers, like to flirt with all the girls!
13   Including my girlfriend!
14 CALEB: True, but has Callie dumped you to go out with me?
15 MASON: Not yet.
16 CALEB: Not yet? *(Smiles.)* Think she might?
17 MASON: Just do me a favor, Caleb. Stay away from Callie!
18 CALEB: But all the girls love me. They all want to confide in me.
19   I can't help that.
20 MASON: Then why don't you just try giving advice to the single
21   girls, not the ones who are taken?
22 CALEB: But it's the ones who are taken that need my advice.
23   And I'm happy to oblige.
24 MASON: Well, just stop obliging my girlfriend, or whatever it is
25   you're doing.
26 CALEB: Mason, if Callie loves you, she'll still come back to you.

1   MASON: But I don't want her hanging out with you!

2   CALEB: *(Waving his arms)* Like a butterfly, she'll fly back to you.

3   But ... if she leaves you for me, then your love wasn't real.

4   MASON: If she leaves me for you, it's because you've confused

5   her with all your so-called advice.

6   CALEB: I only speak the truth. Like, "Baby, you're beautiful.

7   You're perfect in every way. And I love hanging out with

8   you. In fact, let's hang out tonight, OK?" Girls love to hear

9   that stuff. Heck, my phone rings all the time. Especially

10   after one of them has had a big fight with her boyfriend.

11   I'm there to comfort.

12 MASON: So, has Callie ever called you?

13 CALEB: I cannot tell a lie.

14 MASON: Tell me, Caleb! Now!

15 CALEB: Of course she's called me. But only after the two of you

16   have gotten into a fight and she needed a friend. You

17   know, she tells me you're the jealous type. And I can see

18   that she's right.

19 MASON: So Callie's been calling you?

20 CALEB: *(Nods.)* To cry on my shoulder.

21 MASON: Caleb, what if you were in a serious relationship and

22   someone was trying to move in on your girl?

23 CALEB: Remember the butterfly. Let it go, and if it's yours ...

24   Besides, I'm not the kind of guy to be tied down. I prefer

25   to be available for all those hurting young ladies. It's my

26   gift. And they love to cry on this shoulder.

27 MASON: And you love that, don't you?

28 CALEB: *(Smiles.)* I cannot tell a lie. And poor Callie, she's really

29   tired of your jealousy.

30 MASON: Then quit flirting with Callie and I'll quit being

31   jealous!

32 CALEB: Think of the butterfly. Let her go and see what

33   happens.

34 MASON: How about I think of a roach and stomp it dead with

35   my shoe? *(Demonstrates.)*

1   **CALEB: Ouch.**

2   **MASON: Then smear its guts all over the floor!** *(Demonstrates.)*

3   **CALEB: Whoa! No need to overreact!**

4   **MASON: And stomp it again! And again! And again!**

5   *(Demonstrates.)* **Just to make sure!**

6   **CALEB: Look, I'm not the violent type.**

7   **MASON: And I hate roaches! So I love to hear their nasty shell**

8   **crack under my power!** *(Demonstrates.)*

9   **CALEB: You know, I don't have to talk to Callie anymore.**

10   **Because she is a butterfly ... a beautiful butterfly who**

11   **flutters to you ... her one and only boyfriend.**

12 **MASON: Her boyfriend who doesn't like pesty insects getting in**

13   **her path, understand?**

14 **CALEB: Got it. No problem. No problem at all. So I'm just going**

15   **to head back to the cafeteria for some lunch.** *(Starts to*

16   *leave.)*

17 **MASON: And remember ...** *(Stomps his foot, twisting his shoe*

18   *back and forth.)*

19 **CALEB: Gotcha.** *(As he exits)* **I don't want to die!**

39. Progress Report

Cast: BLAKE, JESSE
Props: Paper, pen.
Setting: A classroom.

1 (*AT RISE: BLAKE and JESSE are sitting at desks in a*
2 *classroom.*)
3 **BLAKE: Hey, can you write pretty?**
4 **JESSE: Can I write pretty? Are you kidding me?**
5 **BLAKE: You know, like a girl.**
6 **JESSE: Why?**
7 **BLAKE: Because I need you to do something for me.**
8 **JESSE: Oh, as a joke or something? No problem.** (*Writes.*) **How's**
9   **this?**
10 **BLAKE: Not bad, but try it with more of those curly thingies ...**
11   **you know?**
12 **JESSE: OK.** (*Writes.*) **How's this?**
13 **BLAKE: That's good. Really good. OK, now try writing "Mrs.**
14   **Johnson."**
15 **JESSE: What? Your mom's name?**
16 **BLAKE: Yep. And see if you can do it with those curly thingies**
17   **in her name.**
18 **JESSE: OK.** (*Writes.*) **How's that?**
19 **BLAKE: Great!** (*Puts a piece of paper on JESSE's desk.*) **Now sign**
20   **this.**
21 **JESSE: Your progress report?**
22 **BLAKE: Just sign it.**
23 **JESSE: Wow! This is bad!**
24 **BLAKE: I know! That's why I need *you* to sign it!**
25 **JESSE: I can see that.**
26 **BLAKE:** (*Pointing*) **"Mrs. Johnson," right here.**

1   JESSE: *(Hands the paper back to him.)* **Sorry, but I can't.**

2   **BLAKE: What do you mean, you can't?**

3   JESSE: *(Takes out his progress report.)* **Maybe it's not such a bad**

4   **idea, after all. Mine's not too good, either.**

5   **BLAKE: Then I'll sign "Mrs. Richards" and you sign "Mrs.**

6   **Johnson."**

7   **JESSE: You better practice writing like a girl first.**

8   **BLAKE: OK.** *(Writes.)* **How's that?**

9   **JESSE: Not that great.**

10 **BLAKE:** *(Writes.)* **Better?**

11 **JESSE: Not really. You need more of those curly lines like you**

12   **had me do. Try making a little circle over the "I" instead**

13   **of just a dot. Girls are always doing that.**

14 **BLAKE: Even your mom?**

15 **JESSE: I don't know. I never paid any attention to my mom's**

16   **writing.**

17 **BLAKE:** *(Writes.)* **How's this?**

18 **JESSE: OK, I guess.**

19 **BLAKE: Then let's do this.** *(They swap progress reports.)*

20 **JESSE: Wait! Are you sure we should do this?**

21 **BLAKE: Do you want to die? Because I sure don't. And yours**

22   **may not be as bad as mine, but it is bad.**

23 **JESSE: I know. OK, let's do it.** *(They sign the reports and then*

24   *exchange them.)*

25 **BLAKE:** *(Staring at the report)* **This doesn't look like my mom's**

26   **signature.**

27 **JESSE: This doesn't look like my mom's signature, either. But**

28   **do they even check to see if it matches?**

29 **BLAKE: Nah. They don't have time for that.**

30 **JESSE: But what about this note at the bottom?**

31 **BLAKE: What are you talking about?**

32 **JESSE: If your child has a grade lower than seventy, please call**

33   **the office for a conference. Our moms won't be calling.**

34 **BLAKE: I'm sure a lot of parents don't call.**

35 **JESSE: My mom would call. In fact, she'd be calling the minute**

1   she saw this. And if the office was closed, she'd leave a
2   message, e-mail the teacher, and be the first one in the
3   door the following morning.

4   BLAKE: OK, so we didn't think this through completely.

5   JESSE: And what if our teachers call our moms to set up a
6   conference since they hadn't heard from them?

7   BLAKE: Do you think?

8   JESSE: I don't know. Maybe. But if they do and they find out
9   during the conference that we forged their signatures,
10   we'll probably get suspended from school.

11   BLAKE: OK, so maybe this wasn't such a great idea.

12   JESSE: Yeah, well it's too late now. Unless ...

13   BLAKE: Unless what?

14   JESSE: We white out the signatures and come up with some
15   excuse.

16   BLAKE: Like what? "Sorry mom, I forged your name, but then
17   got scared and covered it up"?

18   JESSE: I didn't say the truth, I said an excuse.

19   BLAKE: OK, smart guy, any suggestions?

20   JESSE: Let's see ... I know!

21   BLAKE: What?

22   JESSE: We'll tell our teacher that we lost our progress reports
23   and ask for another. And believe me, they'll be happy to
24   provide another copy to us.

25   BLAKE: That's true. (*Looks at his report.*) But I'm still tempted
26   to take my chances. My mom is going to kill me.

27   JESSE: Well, I'm going to say I lost mine. I don't want to get
28   suspended. So, what are you going to do?

29   BLAKE: (*Staring at the report*) I'm thinking about it. You know,
30   you do write pretty.

31   JESSE: Thanks. So ... what are you going to do?

32   BLAKE: (*Tears up the report.*) Say I lost it.

33   JESSE: Smart choice.

34   BLAKE: Until my mom sees it. Then it's ... (*Motions cutting*
35   *across the throat.*)

40. Overslept

Cast: AARON, DANNY
Props: Backpacks.
Setting: School hallway.

1　*(AT RISE: AARON enters, his hair a mess, clothes*
2　*mismatched, shirt inside out, and barefoot.)*
3　DANNY: Hey, Aaron, what happened to you?
4　AARON: I overslept. And I can't afford another tardy so I
5　　jumped out of bed and here I am.
6　DANNY: I see that.
7　AARON: You can tell?
8　DANNY: You know, you could've at least brushed your hair. And
9　　I don't know if you noticed, but your shirt is on inside out.
10　AARON: Dang! Well, I guess it doesn't matter as long as I get to
11　　class on time.
12　DANNY: Well, my friend, you may look a bit run over, but you
13　　made it. *(Looks at watch.)* With a few minutes to spare.
14　AARON: *(Smoothes down hair.)* And I was having a good dream
15　　when I realized I had fifteen minutes to get to school.
16　DANNY: Bet you didn't eat breakfast, did you?
17　AARON: No, and I'm hungry. You have anything?
18　DANNY: Uh, I might. *(Sets backpack on the floor, then kneels*
19　　*down and digs through it.)* Uh, Aaron, I think you forgot
20　　something.
21　AARON: What?
22　DANNY: Your shoes.
23　AARON: What? *(Looks down at his feet.)* Oh, great! How did I do
24　　that?
25　DANNY: How did you not notice? Didn't you feel a strange
26　　sensation when you ran across the school parking lot?

1   Like gravel or glass piercing your skin?

2   AARON: Man! I was in such a hurry to get to school that I didn't

3   even feel a thing! What am I going to do now? The first

4   teacher who notices my bare feet is going to send me

5   home.

6   DANNY: True, but you won't get a tardy if you're sent home.

7   AARON: Not a tardy, but an unexcused absence! Again! Then it's

8   detention!

9   DANNY: Maybe none of the teachers will notice.

10   AARON: Are you serious? Have you ever had Mrs. Love?

11   DANNY: Never mind.

12   AARON: And believe me, she's usually not feeling the love at all.

13   It's all about following the rules in her class. Yesterday she

14   sent Ryan to the office for having a small tear in his jeans.

15   And we're talking small.

16   DANNY: Wow. That's not good. I don't think any of my teachers

17   would notice or care, but Mrs. Love ...

18   AARON: She's going to have a fit when she sees me. She'll

19   probably say that my feet stink, too!

20   DANNY: *(Laughs.)* That's funny. Sorry.

21   AARON: Too bad I can't borrow a pair of shoes just for her class.

22   DANNY: Yeah, really.

23   AARON: Uh, Danny ...

24   DANNY: No!

25   AARON: Come on! Just for Mrs. Love's class? You know I

26   wouldn't ask if she wasn't going to cause this big ugly

27   scene, embarrass me, and send me to the office. Please!

28   DANNY: I don't know ...

29   AARON: Come on, I'd do it for you. And it's just for this one

30   class. All my other teachers are cool and either won't

31   notice or won't care.

32   DANNY: Danny, I don't know ...

33   AARON: What do you have first period?

34   DANNY: Drama.

35   AARON: That's great! You know Mr. Sikes won't care if you

1   come into class without wearing shoes. He'll probably tell
2   you that you're being bold or uninhibited or something
3   cool like that.
4 DANNY: Yeah, probably.
5 AARON: So, come on! Let me borrow your shoes before the bell
6   rings!
7 DANNY: You know, I'm going to feel really weird walking into
8   class without any shoes.
9 AARON: No one will even notice. And you could do something
10   to draw all the attention up. You know, some of your
11   stupid imitations.
12 DANNY: Thanks, Aaron.
13 AARON: I don't mean stupid. I mean funny.
14 DANNY: Are you sure you mean funny and not stupid?
15 AARON: Come on, the bell's about to ring!
16 DANNY: *(Takes off shoes.)* And you'll meet me back here after
17   first period, right?
18 AARON: *(Puts on shoes.)* Hey, I like these!
19 DANNY: Right here after first period, right?
20 AARON: These are cool. I like them.
21 DANNY: Hey, don't be stinking them all up!
22 AARON: I need to get a pair like these.
23 DANNY: My feet are cold.
24 AARON: *(Jogging in place)* I think I could run really fast in
25   these.
26 DANNY: I feel stupid.
27 AARON: Hey, there's the bell! Gotta go! Thanks, Danny! Bye!
28   *(Runs off.)*
29 DANNY: *(Hollering)* Remember to meet me back here after first
30   period, OK? *(Looks down at his feet, shakes his head, and*
31   *exits.)*

Men and Women

41. Fundraiser

Cast: DAVID, EMILY
Props: Toilet paper.
Setting: School hallway, outside a bathroom.

1   *(AT RISE: EMILY is standing in a hallway, holding a sack of*
2   *toilet paper. DAVID walks past her.)*
3   **EMILY:** *(Quickly holding out a roll of toilet paper)* **Hey, do you**
4   **want to buy a roll of toilet paper?**
5   **DAVID:** *(Turning)* **Who, me?**
6   **EMILY: Yes. So, do you? Want to buy a roll of toilet paper?**
7   **DAVID: Uh, not really.**
8   **EMILY: But it's for a good cause. The band is earning money for**
9   **our spring trip to Hawaii.**
10 **DAVID: By selling toilet paper?**
11 **EMILY: Actually we're selling cases of toilet paper, but I**
12 **thought I could make more money by selling it by the roll.**
13 **DAVID: I'm afraid to ask, but how much is a roll?**
14 **EMILY: Only a dollar.**
15 **DAVID:** *Only a dollar?* **You can practically buy four rolls for a**
16 **dollar.**
17 **EMILY: It's for a good cause.**
18 **DAVID: So you can go to Hawaii.**
19 **EMILY:** *(Attempts to hula dance.)* **Can't wait! It will be the best trip**
20 **ever! But I still need a thousand dollars, which means ...**
21 **DAVID: You have to sell a thousand rolls of toilet paper.**
22 **EMILY:** *(Determined)* **And I'm going to do it!**
23 **DAVID: How many have you sold?**
24 **EMILY: Three.**
25 **DAVID: Wow. You've got a long way to go.**
26 **EMILY: Yes, but I'm determined. So, how many rolls would you**

1   like to buy?

2   DAVID: Well, if you were selling candy bars, I'd buy a couple of

3   those. But toilet paper? I don't think so.

4   EMILY: Please!

5   DAVID: Sorry, but I don't want to buy any toilet paper. And

6   wouldn't I look stupid walking down the hall carrying

7   toilet paper?

8   EMILY: You could put it in your backpack or your locker.

9   DAVID: Look, I can go to the bathroom and get all the free toilet

10   paper I want.

11   EMILY: If there's any in there.

12   DAVID: What?

13   EMILY: *(Pointing)* If there's any toilet paper in there. And don't

14   you just hate to go to the bathroom, sit down, and then

15   realize the roll is empty? I hate that. Of course, if you're

16   lucky, someone in the stall next to you might hand you

17   some, but if there's not anyone there ... you're in trouble.

18   Yuck.

19   DAVID: Wait a minute! Are you telling me that there's no toilet

20   paper to be found in any of the bathrooms?

21   EMILY: I didn't say that.

22   DAVID: You stole all the toilet paper out of the bathrooms so

23   you can earn money to go to Hawaii?

24   EMILY: I didn't say that, either.

25   DAVID: So, if I go into the boys' bathroom right here, I'll find

26   plenty of toilet paper?

27   EMILY: Uh ... I wouldn't say that, either.

28   DAVID: *(Runs into the bathroom, then back out.)* You did! You

29   stole all the toilet paper!

30   EMILY: How do you know? You didn't see me steal all the toilet

31   paper.

32   DAVID: No, but since you're standing outside the bathroom

33   with a sack full of toilet paper that you're trying to sell for

34   a dollar a roll, I'd say the odds are very good! And by the

35   way, how did you get into the boys' bathroom?

1   EMILY: I'm not admitting anything.
2   DAVID: And you think you can get away with this?
3   EMILY: Look, I want to go to Hawaii!
4   DAVID: And I want to go to the bathroom and have some toilet
5   paper on the roll!
6   EMILY: *(Holds out a roll.)* It's only a dollar.
7   DAVID: You know what? If the principal finds out that you stole
8   all the toilet paper in the bathrooms and you're trying to sell
9   it for a dollar a roll, I don't think you'll be going to Hawaii.
10 EMILY: Oh! I didn't think about that!
11 DAVID: Sell candy. That goes like crazy. Especially during third
12   period before lunch. Heck, you could even double the
13   price. Because at that time of the day, I'd pay just about
14   anything for a chocolate bar.
15 EMILY: That's a good idea.
16 DAVID: And you better get rid of all that toilet paper before you
17   get caught.
18 EMILY: You know, you're right. I don't want to get into trouble
19   and not get to go on my trip. Hey, would you do me a favor?
20 DAVID: Forget it.
21 EMILY: Please! I had enough trouble getting in there and I sure
22   don't want to go back.
23 DAVID: Oh, just give it to me! *(She hands him the rolls.)* And
24   tomorrow I better find you selling candy bars instead!
25 EMILY: Thanks. Are you going to buy one from me?
26 DAVID: I don't know. How much is it going to cost me?
27 EMILY: Five dollars?
28 DAVID: Five dollars for a candy bar?
29 EMILY: You said I should double my price.
30 DAVID: And I think you should give me a discount.
31 EMILY: Why would I do that?
32 DAVID: For putting all your toilet paper back in the boys'
33   bathroom!
34 EMILY: OK, two-fifty and the candy bar is yours. *(DAVID shakes*
35   *his head and disappears into the boys' bathroom.)*

42. Parking Permit

Cast: JACOB, MRS. COOK
Props: Car keys, driver's license,
insurance card, cash, paper and pen.
Setting: School office.

1   *(AT RISE: JACOB approaches MRS. COOK, who is standing*
2   *behind a counter.)*
3   **MRS. COOK: May I help you?**
4   **JACOB:** *(Proudly)* **Yes, ma'am!** *(Rattles his car keys.)* **I need to buy**
5   **a parking permit.**
6   **MRS. COOK:** *(Coldly)* **First car?**
7   **JACOB:** *(Takes out his driver's license.)* **Got my license yesterday.**
8   **MRS. COOK: Great. Another sixteen-year-old driver on the**
9   **streets. God help us all.**
10   **JACOB: But I'm a good driver!**
11   **MRS. COOK:** *(Mimics him.)* **"But I'm a good driver." And you've**
12   **been driving for how long?**
13   **JACOB: By myself? Well, this is my first day.**
14   **MRS. COOK: Uh-huh.** *(Suddenly)* ***Slam! Bam! Crash!***
15   **JACOB: Excuse me?**
16   **MRS. COOK: Won't be long! See it all the time. First car ... Slam!**
17   **Bam! Crash!**
18   **JACOB: No, really, I'm a good driver.**
19   **MRS. COOK:** *(Mimics.)* **"But I'm a good driver." Do you know**
20   **how many students have told me that? And do you know**
21   **how many of those students have wrecked their first car?**
22   **JACOB: A couple?**
23   **MRS. COOK:** *(Laughs.)* **A couple? A couple? Try a couple**
24   **hundred!**
25   **JACOB: This year?**

1　MRS. COOK: No, not this year, but over the past several years. A
2　　　sixteen-year-old gets his first license, and then it's slam,
3　　　bam, crash!
4　JACOB: *(Rattling his keys)* Well, not me! *(Confident)* I'm a good
5　　　driver.
6　MRS. COOK: Uh-huh. Right. OK, fill out this form please. And
7　　　I'll need to see your proof of insurance.
8　JACOB: *(Takes out his insurance card.)* No problem.
9　MRS. COOK: You realize your insurance will double in price
10　　　after your first wreck, don't you?
11　JACOB: Well, I'm not going to have a wreck. Like I told you, I'm
12　　　a good driver.
13　MRS. COOK: Sure, sure. After one day of driving alone you
14　　　think you're a good driver? Please! *(Begins laughing again.)*
15　　　Just take my advice and don't speed. I know how you
16　　　teenagers are.
17　JACOB: I don't speed.
18　MRS. COOK: *(Shakes head.)* I'm warning you, it won't be long.
19　JACOB: Here. *(Hands her the form.)* So, do you try to scare
20　　　everyone that comes into the office to buy their first
21　　　parking permit?
22　MRS. COOK: I'm sorry. Was I scaring you?
23　JACOB: Well, no ... I'm not scared.
24　MRS. COOK: Listen, I'm just telling you what I see. And I see
25　　　sixteen-year-olds wrecking their cars right and left. By the
26　　　way, what street do you take to go home? Because I need to
27　　　add that to my list.
28　JACOB: Your list?
29　MRS. COOK: *(Takes out a piece of paper.)* Street?
30　JACOB: University.
31　MRS. COOK: Oh, good. That's already on my list of streets to
32　　　avoid.
33　JACOB: Excuse me?
34　MRS. COOK: I zigzag home every day to avoid all the
35　　　inexperienced drivers.

1   JACOB: So, how many wrecks have you had, Mrs. Cook?

2   MRS. COOK: Me? Zero. But about a hundred close calls in the
3   school parking lot. And that's why I started waiting until
4   everyone is gone before I leave.

5   JACOB: Well, you don't have to worry about me. Can I have my
6   permit now?

7   MRS. COOK: That'll be thirty-five dollars. *(He gives her the*
8   *money.)* And please, please try to remember all those
9   things you learned in Driver's Education.

10   JACOB: Well, that'll be hard since I practically slept through the
11   class.

12   MRS. COOK: *What?*

13   JACOB: And I barely passed the test. *(Rattles his keys.)* But I
14   passed! Yeah!

15   MRS. COOK: *(Takes out her street list again.)* And what other
16   streets will you be traveling on?

17   JACOB: What streets? Well, I'll be all over the place. Cruising.
18   Racing ...

19   MRS. COOK: Oh, no!

20   JACOB: So you better look out! Because I just got my driver's
21   license! *Yes! (Exits.)*

43. Friends to Lovers

Cast: JASON, ALLISON
Props: Twenty-five folded notes.
Setting: School hallway.

1 **JASON: Hey, Allison! Wait up!**

2 **ALLISON: Hi, Jason. What's up?**

3 **JASON: Here. I wrote you a couple of notes during school today.**

4 *(Hands her twenty-four of the notes.)*

5 **ALLISON: A couple?**

6 **JASON: I always get finished with my work early, so I have time**

7 **to do what I want. And I wanted to write to you!**

8 **ALLISON: *(Attempting to hold all the notes)* But why so many?**

9 **JASON: Oh, wait! I forgot one! *(Digs into his pocket and pulls out***

10 *another folded note.)* **Here. I probably shouldn't tell you**

11 **this since I told you in most of the notes, but ... well ... well,**

12 **maybe I shouldn't tell you.**

13 **ALLISON: *(Frustrated)* What, Jason? Tell me! Because it might**

14 **take all night to read all these notes!**

15 **JASON: *(Smiles.)* I'm glad you want to read my notes. Because**

16 **today, I've spelled it all out. Or is that spilled it all out?**

17 **ALLISON: What are you talking about?**

18 **JASON: My feelings. Right there. In those notes.**

19 **ALLISON: Your feelings? What feelings?**

20 **JASON: Well ...**

21 **ALLISON: Yes?**

22 **JASON: Allison ...**

23 **ALLISON: Yes?**

24 **JASON: I'm really glad we're friends.**

25 **ALLISON: OK. Me, too.**

26 **JASON: And tonight when you're reading all my notes, you'll**

1   understand how I *really* feel.

2 ALLISON: About?

3 JASON: I'm not saying another word. I don't want to spoil the

4   surprise ...

5 ALLISON: What surprise?

6 JASON: You'll see.

7 ALLISON: Jason!

8 JASON: You'll have to wait and read about it tonight ... well,

9   about me ... actually, about us.

10 ALLISON: Jason, I don't have time to read all these notes

11   tonight! I've got homework.

12 JASON: But Allison, you have to! I understand it's a lot to read,

13   but it's important!

14 ALLISON: But Jason, there are so many notes here! And I've got

15   to write a paper about nineteenth century philosophy!

16 JASON: And look! I numbered all the notes so you'll know what

17   order to read them. One through twenty-five.

18 ALLISON: How about if I just read the last one first? You know,

19   get to the punch line.

20 JASON: No, no, you can't do that! That's the best one! You have

21   to save it for last!

22 ALLISON: Why?

23 JASON: Because all my notes are leading up to that last one! It's

24   the most important one of them all! So save the last note

25   for last! OK? Promise?

26 ALLISON: I guess, but ... Jason, why don't you just give me a hint

27   about what's in the last note?

28 JASON: No, I can't. I just can't.

29 ALLISON: Come on, Jason.

30 JASON: Well, it's about us.

31 ALLISON: Us? What about us? We've been friends since

32   kindergarten. We live next door to each other. We're great

33   friends. What else is there to say?

34 JASON: There's much more to say, Allison. Much, much more.

35 ALLISON: But what's so important about the last note? Tell me.

1 JASON: I can't. I just can't.

2 ALLISON: Why not?

3 JASON: Because I'm afraid to tell you. I'm afraid of your

4   reaction. That's why I wrote it all down.

5 ALLISON: Now you're scaring me!

6 JASON: I'm sorry. Just read the notes. Start with the first one,

7   and by the time you get to the twenty-fifth one, maybe

8   you'll understand.

9 ALLISON: Jason, just tell me! Tell me right now!

10 JASON: OK, OK! *(Deep breath)* Allison, I don't want to be your

11   friend anymore.

12 ALLISON: You don't want to be my friend anymore? And it took

13   you twenty-five notes to say that?

14 JASON: No, no! Not that I don't want to be your friend anymore,

15   but that I want to be *more* than just your friend.

16 ALLISON: More than just my friend? *(He nods.)* As in boyfriend-

17   girlfriend kind of thing? *(He nods. Long pause)* I see. Well,

18   tonight I'll write you back.

19 JASON: And tell me what an idiot I am! Tell me how I've ruined

20   everything and how stupid I am!

21 ALLISON: And it'll only take me one note to say what I have to

22   say.

23 JASON: You hate me.

24 ALLISON: No, I don't hate you.

25 JASON: *(Attempting to take the notes from her)* Allison, I take it

26   all back! Tomorrow we'll go back to being just friends,

27   OK?

28 ALLISON: Jason, I was going to write that I wish you had told

29   me sooner.

30 JASON: Why? So you could've set me straight before I ruined

31   our friendship?

32 ALLISON: No, because we've wasted so much time.

33 JASON: We have?

34 ALLISON: And you know what they say about friends.

35 JASON: *(Smiling)* Friends make the best lovers?

1   ALLISON: Now, give me those notes back. I'm going to read
2   every single one of them!
3   JASON: Are you going to write me back?
4   ALLISON: How about if you just come over instead?
5   JASON: Yeah, that'd be great!
6   ALLISON: *(As they are walking off)* And tonight you can help me
7   write that paper.
8   JASON: My pleasure! Nineteenth century philosophy? What's
9   that all about?
10 ALLISON: I don't have a clue.

44. I.O.U.

Cast: MR. LEWIS, HANNAH
Props: Cell phones, pen, paper.
Setting: A classroom.

1   *(AT RISE: MR. LEWIS is sitting at his desk. Several cell*
2   *phones are lined up on his desk. HANNAH enters.)*
3   **HANNAH:** Mr. Lewis, may I please have my cell phone back?
4   **MR. LEWIS:** *(Holds out his hand.)* **Fifteen dollars, please.**
5   **HANNAH: I have to pay to get my phone back?**
6   **MR. LEWIS: New school policy.**
7   **HANNAH: But that's not fair!**
8   **MR. LEWIS: And it's not fair that you disrupted class when your**
9   **phone rang.**
10   **HANNAH: But it wasn't my fault.**
11   **MR. LEWIS:** *(Imitates.)* **"But it wasn't my fault!" Do you know**
12   **how tired I am of hearing that?** *(Imitates.)* **"It wasn't my**
13   **fault!" And whose fault do you think it was?**
14   **HANNAH: I mean it wasn't my fault that someone called me. All**
15   **my friends who call me were in school so I don't know**
16   **why it rang. And I didn't answer it!**
17   **MR. LEWIS: The point is, it rang and disrupted my class. No**
18   **phones are allowed in the classroom. New school policy.**
19   *(Holds out his hand.)* **Fifteen dollars, please.**
20   **HANNAH: But I don't have fifteen dollars.**
21   **MR. LEWIS:** *(Imitates.)* **"But I don't have fifteen dollars!" Then I**
22   **guess you don't get your phone back, do you?**
23   **HANNAH: Wait! Any chance I could write you an I.O.U.? I'll**
24   **bring you the money tomorrow!**
25   **MR. LEWIS: Sorry, but no I.O.U.s.**
26   **HANNAH: But ...**

1 MR. LEWIS: If you can't pay, then you're wasting my time.

2 HANNAH: Please, Mr. Lewis! I'll pay you tomorrow, OK?

3 MR. LEWIS: That's fine.

4 HANNAH: It is?

5 MR. LEWIS: Of course. Pay me tomorrow, day after tomorrow,
6   next week, next month ...

7 HANNAH: But you'll give me my phone back today?

8 MR. LEWIS: *(Holds out his hand.)* Fifteen dollars, please.

9 HANNAH: But I don't have fifteen dollars! Please, let me write
10   you an I.O.U.! I'll pay you tomorrow! I promise!

11 MR. LEWIS: Promises, promises, promises ...

12 HANNAH: Mr. Lewis, I'll *die* if I don't have my phone back!

13 MR. LEWIS: *(Laughs.)* I highly doubt that.

14 HANNAH: I have to call Bryan after school and I don't have his
15   number memorized because it's programmed into my
16   phone! That's why I need my phone! So I can call him!

17 MR. LEWIS: Maybe that was him calling you during class.

18 HANNAH: No, because we never talk until after school. It was
19   probably a wrong number.

20 MR. LEWIS: Not my fault.

21 HANNAH: Please, Mr. Lewis, please! Let me write you an I.O.U.!
22   I'll do it right now! *(Finds paper and pen and writes*
23   *furiously.)* "I.O.U. fifteen dollars. Signed Hannah
24   Ellsworth." *(Hands him the paper.)*

25 MR. LEWIS: Not acceptable. Sorry.

26 HANNAH: But please! Please! *(Gets on her knees.)*

27 MR. LEWIS: *(Watches for a moment.)* This is a first. You're
28   begging?

29 HANNAH: Mr. Lewis, I'm begging you, begging you for my
30   phone!

31 MR. LEWIS: *(Picks up her phone and looks at it.)* This is a nice
32   phone. Do your parents realize that you take it to school?

33 HANNAH: Mr. Lewis, everyone takes their phone to school.

34 MR. LEWIS: But not everyone's phone rings during class. Ever
35   heard of vibrate?

1   HANNAH: I thought it was on vibrate!
2   MR. LEWIS: And I bet next time you'll be more careful, won't
3   you? Not that I'm telling you to bring your phone to class ...
4   HANNAH: Mr. Lewis, I'll never let it ring again! I promise!
5   MR. LEWIS: And I guess you want your phone back, don't you?
6   HANNAH: Yes! Please!
7   MR. LEWIS: (Holds out his hand.) Fifteen dollars, please.
8   HANNAH: (Places the I.O.U. in his hand.) And I'll pay you first
9   thing in the morning, OK?
10 MR. LEWIS: Because you have to call Bobby or Billy or someone
11   like that?
12 HANNAH: Bryan!
13 MR. LEWIS: Just curious, but what do you need to tell Bryan
14   that's so important?
15 HANNAH: Mr. Lewis, that's personal!
16 MR. LEWIS: I don't mind.
17 HANNAH: Mr. Lewis!
18 MR. LEWIS: All right, all right. Well, you need to add one more
19   thing to this I.O.U.
20 HANNAH: What?
21 MR. LEWIS: Plus interest.
22 HANNAH: You're charging me interest?
23 MR. LEWIS: That's right.
24 HANNAH: Can you do that?
25 MR. LEWIS: No one said I couldn't.
26 HANNAH: (Grabs paper and writes.) Plus interest. (Hands him
27   the paper.)
28 MR. LEWIS: Thank you. (Hands her the phone.)
29 HANNAH: (Sigh of relief) Thank you. Oh, thank you. And I'll get
30   the money from my mother tonight. But how much extra?
31   I mean, how much will it be for the interest you're
32   charging me?
33 MR. LEWIS: (Smiles.) One hundred math problems. Due by
34   tomorrow. (Gives her a work sheet.) Here you go!

45. The Break-Up

Cast: JUSTIN, ASHLEY

1   JUSTIN: Ashley, I'm sorry.

2   ASHLEY: Sorry? Sorry?

3   JUSTIN: Look it's not you, it's me.

4   ASHLEY: Of course it's me!

5   JUSTIN: No, no, you're great.

6   ASHLEY: If I were so great, you wouldn't be dumping me. So,

7   who is she?

8   JUSTIN: Who?

9   ASHLEY: *Her!* The girl you're dumping me for!

10   JUSTIN: Ashley, there is no one else. It's just ...

11   ASHLEY: What? Tell me!

12   JUSTIN: I don't think I'm ready for a serious relationship.

13   ASHLEY: And it took you fourteen months to figure that out?

14   JUSTIN: *(Shrugs.)* I need some space.

15   ASHLEY: To do what? Sit at home alone?

16   JUSTIN: I don't know. Hang out with the guys, I guess.

17   ASHLEY: Well, Justin, all your guy friends have girlfriends!

18   JUSTIN: Well, that's true.

19   ASHLEY: So, what's her name?

20   JUSTIN: Her name?

21   ASHLEY: Tell me!

22   JUSTIN: There is no one else.

23   ASHLEY: Justin, you better tell me because I'm about to find

24   her and pull out every strand of her hair!

25   JUSTIN: Ashley, there's no one else! I just don't feel like being

26   tied down. I feel like I need to breathe.

1 ASHLEY: And you can't breathe around me?

2 JUSTIN: I need a break.

3 ASHLEY: Oh, you are such a jerk! Fourteen months together

4   and then you break up! Oh! I hate you, Justin!

5 JUSTIN: Can't we still be friends?

6 ASHLEY: Friends? *Friends?*

7 JUSTIN: Sure, why not?

8 ASHLEY: Sure, if you'll tell me her name.

9 JUSTIN: There is no name to tell.

10 ASHLEY: Liar.

11 JUSTIN: It's the truth!

12 ASHLEY: Then give me her initials.

13 JUSTIN: Her initials? For a girl who doesn't exist?

14 ASHLEY: Tell me! Tell me those two little letters this very

15   second or I'm going to scream!

16 JUSTIN: Uh ...

17 ASHLEY: *Tell me!*

18 JUSTIN: OK. M.A.

19 ASHLEY: M.A.? *(He nods. Trying to figure out who this is, she*

20   *repeats the letters.)* **M.A. M.A. M.A.** *(Finally)* **Melanie**

21   **Anderson?**

22 JUSTIN: Who's that? I don't even know a Melanie Anderson.

23 ASHLEY: M.A. *(Thinking)* Madison Archer?

24 JUSTIN: Madison Archer? No way! Yuck!

25 ASHLEY: Then who? I can't think of anyone else with those

26   initials.

27 JUSTIN: That's because there is no one else.

28 ASHLEY: Then what about the initials?

29 JUSTIN: I made them up so you wouldn't scream at me.

30 ASHLEY: Then what did M.A. stand for?

31 JUSTIN: *(Smiles.)* **Miss America.** *(ASHLEY screams.)*

46. Sole Student

Cast: CONNER, MRS. MORRIS
Props: Attendance book, paper and pen
Setting: A classroom.

1 *(AT RISE: MRS. MORRIS is sitting at her desk. CONNER*
2 *enters and sits at a desk. After a moment, he looks around*
3 *the room, wondering why he's the only student in the*
4 *classroom.)*
5 **MRS. MORRIS:** *(Stands, speaking to the classroom as if there*
6 *were more than one student.)* **Welcome! Welcome back to**
7 **the first day of school! This class, Growing the Perfect**
8 **Tomato, is a new elective this year, and I'm so pleased that**
9 **you've signed up for it. Now, let's get started.**
10 **CONNER:** *(Raises hand.)* **Uh ... Where's everyone else?**
11 **MRS. MORRIS: Well, it looks like you're it.**
12 **CONNER: I'm it? You mean I'm the *only* student in this class?**
13 **MRS. MORRIS: I guess Growing the Perfect Tomato wasn't as**
14 **popular as I'd imagined it would be. But that's all right.**
15 **You're here.**
16 **CONNER: But don't they usually cancel a class if there are not**
17 **enough students signed up?**
18 **MRS. MORRIS: Not necessarily. And besides, I don't mind**
19 **having just one student. One, thirty ... it doesn't matter to**
20 **me. I'm here to teach.**
21 **CONNER: But ... I didn't even sign up for this tomato class. I**
22 **don't even like tomatoes.**
23 **MRS. MORRIS:** *(Checks her attendance book.)* **Well, you're on my**
24 **list, which means you must have signed up.**
25 **CONNER: But I didn't! It must've been a computer glitch!**
26 **MRS. MORRIS:** *(Holding up her attendance book)* **OK, let's get**

1   started by checking the roll. Conner Davis.

2   CONNER: *(Takes a deep breath. Raises hand.)* **Here.**

3   MRS. MORRIS: *(Shuts book.)* **Good. All right, let's begin with the**
4   **rules of my classroom. First and foremost, no talking**
5   **during class.**

6   CONNER: *(Raises hand.)* **Uh ... who am I going to talk to?**

7   MRS. MORRIS: *(Ignoring him)* **And of course there's the rule of**
8   **no cheating. And let me just say this. If I catch you even**
9   **glancing at your neighbor's paper, it will be an automatic**
10   **zero.**

11   CONNER: *(Raises hand.)* **Uh ...**

12   MRS. MORRIS: **Growing the Perfect Tomato can be a difficult**
13   **subject, and I want you to know that I'm here for you at all**
14   **times. So, if you're having problems understanding what**
15   **we're doing, then tutoring is available before and after**
16   **school.**

17   CONNER: *(Raises hand.)* **May I go to the office?**

18   MRS. MORRIS: **Is this an emergency?**

19   CONNER: **I don't guess it's an emergency, but I was going to see**
20   **about having my schedule changed.**

21   MRS. MORRIS: **There will be no schedule changes.**

22   CONNER: **But ...**

23   MRS. MORRIS: **Now, shall we continue with the rules of my**
24   **class? Are you taking notes? Because you need to be taking**
25   **notes. OK, another rule in my classroom is no food or**
26   **drinks allowed. Unless of course it's a tomato. Tomatoes**
27   **are allowed. And you may eat them as you please. And**
28   **there's no gum, no cell phones and no writing or passing**
29   **notes during my class. Any questions?**

30   CONNER: *(Raises hand.)* **Uh ... is it required that we eat**
31   **tomatoes?**

32   MRS. MORRIS: **Of course it's required that you eat tomatoes!**
33   **How can we know if we're growing the perfect tomato if**
34   **we don't taste the perfect tomato?**

35   CONNER: **But I don't like tomatoes.**

1   **MRS. MORRIS:** Well, I imagine you'd better learn to like
2   tomatoes, then!
3   **CONNER:** *(Raises hand.)* May I please go to the office?
4   **MRS. MORRIS:** Is this an emergency?
5   **CONNER:** Yes, I would say it is.
6   **MRS. MORRIS:** And what is your so-called emergency?
7   **CONNER:** To ask for a schedule change because I hate
8   tomatoes!
9   **MRS. MORRIS:** I'm sorry, but no passes are handed out during
10   my class so you can roam the halls. I expect you to sit up
11   straight and pay attention. Now, for your first assignment ...
12   **CONNER:** Please, tell me we're not going to eat a tomato!
13   **MRS. MORRIS:** How can we? We haven't grown the perfect
14   tomato yet, have we?
15   **CONNER:** No. Thank goodness.
16   **MRS. MORRIS:** Now, for your first assignment, I'd like for you
17   to write an essay about your favorite memory of eating a
18   tomato. Perhaps it was on a picnic with your family or
19   fresh out of the garden with your grandparents ...
20   **CONNER:** What if it's about picking them off my hamburger at
21   McDonalds?
22   **MRS. MORRIS:** *(Glaring at him)* And this will be for a grade!
23   **CONNER:** Mrs. Morris, may I please, *please* go to the office?
24   **MRS. MORRIS:** Look ... *(Checks her attendance book)* Conner
25   Davis ... just because you don't like the class you've been
26   placed in doesn't mean you can run off to the office and
27   whine about it. And as you will quickly learn, growing the
28   perfect tomato is a skill that you will appreciate as you get
29   into adulthood. Now, I suggest that you get started on that
30   assignment.
31   **CONNER:** *(Takes out paper and pen. After a pause, he raises his*
32   *hand.)* Any chance we could learn to grow something else?
33   Because I really, really don't like tomatoes!
34   **MRS. MORRIS:** And I want at least five hundred words!
35   **CONNER:** But ...

1   **MRS. MORRIS: And tomorrow ...** *(Smiles)* **we will sample many**
2   **different types of tomatoes. Yum! Plum tomatoes, Roma**
3   **tomatoes, cherry tomatoes ...**
4   **CONNER: Yuck.**
5   **MRS. MORRIS: And perhaps you already know this, but**
6   **tomatoes are technically a fruit.**
7   **CONNER: Except they don't taste like a fruit.**
8   **MRS. MORRIS: And Americans love tomatoes. In fact, the US**
9   **Department of Agriculture has estimated that the average**
10   **American eats over twenty-two pounds of tomatoes each**
11   **year.**
12   **CONNER: Guess I'm not average.**
13   **MRS. MORRIS: Mostly in the form of ketchup and tomato sauce**
14   **as well as spaghetti sauce, salsa ...**
15   **CONNER: Hey, I love ketchup! And salsa!**
16   **MRS. MORRIS: Then, see, you do love tomatoes after all.**
17   **CONNER: Hey, can we make our own salsa?**
18   **MRS. MORRIS: That's part of what we'll be doing this semester.**
19   **CONNER: Cool! I like that!**
20   **MRS. MORRIS: But first, that essay about your favorite tomato**
21   **experience.**
22   **CONNER:** *(Smiles.)* **Dipping potato chips in ketchup. Yum!**
23   *(Begins writing.)*

47. Plain Jane

Cast: KEVIN, JANE
Props: Old-fashioned hat.

1   *(AT RISE: JANE enters wearing a ridiculous hat.)*

2   **KEVIN: What is this? Hat day?**

3   **JANE:** *(Dramatic)* **It's hat day for me! You like?**

4   **KEVIN: No.**

5   **JANE: It's my new style. A new me!**

6   **KEVIN: Uh ... What was wrong with the old you?**

7   **JANE: The old me was not popular. I was so ... you know ...**

8   **ordinary. Nothing spectacular. Nothing striking. Just**

9   **boring old Jane.**

10   **KEVIN: Well, I like boring old Jane.**

11   **JANE: You and you alone.**

12   **KEVIN: Seriously, Jane, have you looked in the mirror?**

13   **JANE: Of course. Why?**

14   **KEVIN: And you're still planning to enter the school building**

15   **looking like that?**

16   **JANE: Of course. Why not?**

17   **KEVIN: Think about it. How many of our friends do you see**

18   **wearing hats to school? Except on Crazy Hat Day.**

19   **JANE: Well, as you may know, the boys are not allowed to wear**

20   **their hats in the building, but girls are.**

21   **KEVIN: And how many girls do you see wearing hats to school?**

22   **JANE: I'm going to start a new trend! And I bet that tomorrow**

23   **you'll see lots of girls wearing hats to school after I**

24   **introduce this new style. Then before you know it,**

25   **everyone will be wearing hats!**

26   **KEVIN: Yeah, right. So, where did you get that hat?**

1   JANE: The attic. It was my grandmother's hat back in the
2   thirties or forties or something like that. You know, Kevin,
3   back then, women wore hats all the time.
4   KEVIN: Yeah, back then. *Way* back then!
5   JANE: And today, I'm bringing the style back. So, how do I look?
6   KEVIN: Stupid.
7   JANE: What?
8   KEVIN: I'm being honest.
9   JANE: That wasn't a very nice thing to say!
10   KEVIN: I have an idea. Let me see your hat.
11   JANE: Why?
12   KEVIN: Just let me see it. *(She hands the hat to him and he puts*
13   *it on.)* Now, how do I look?
14   JANE: *(Pause as she stares at him.)* Turn around.
15   KEVIN: *(Turns.)* Well?
16   JANE: *(Grabs the hat off his head.)* You look stupid! And I guess
17   I look stupid, too! It was a stupid idea to wear this hat, and
18   I'll never be anything but plain and ordinary. So just call
19   me Plain Jane!
20   KEVIN: It beats getting laughed at, doesn't it?
21   JANE: *(Thinking)* I don't know. It'd be more attention than I'm
22   getting right now. People would say, "Look! Look at that
23   girl over there wearing that hat!"
24   KEVIN: Yes. Everyone would be talking about you.
25   JANE: *(Puts the hat on and smiles.)* Good! Then I'll finally get
26   noticed! And I'll just hold my head up high as if I'm
27   someone special! And I'll walk through the halls with a
28   mysterious look on my face. People who didn't know me
29   before will suddenly want to know who I am. They'll
30   wonder, "Who is that girl wearing that hat?"
31   KEVIN: Maybe they'll wonder if you have a bald head.
32   JANE: No they won't!
33   KEVIN: That's what people do when their hair falls out. Or they
34   totally botched it with a bad haircut.
35   JANE: Well, I'll just tell everyone that it's the new style.

1   KEVIN: Even though all the teen magazines forgot to put hats
2   on the models?
3   JANE: Sure. I'll be ahead of the times. Anticipating the newest
4   and hottest fad.
5   KEVIN: With that old hat? I mean, it might have been stylish
6   back then, but now ... *(Shakes head.)* You look like my
7   grandma.
8   JANE: I don't look like a grandma! I think I look glamorous!
9   *(Holds head up.)* And stylish.
10   KEVIN: Well, there's the bell. You coming?
11   JANE: OK, one more time. How do I look?
12   KEVIN: I told you. You look stupid. *(Exits.)*
13   JANE: No I don't! *(Adjusts hat.)* I look stupendous! *(Holding her*
14   *head high, she walks off.)* Beautiful. Yes, beautiful. I can do
15   this.

48. The Bribe

Cast: CARTER, MRS. MOORE
Props: Apple, trash can, grade book.
Setting: A classroom.

1   *(AT RISE: CARTER enters the room and approaches MRS.*
2   *MOORE.)*
3   **CARTER:** *(Proudly holding out a shiny red apple)* **Here, Mrs.**
4   **Moore, I brought you something!**
5   **MRS. MOORE:** *(Looking down at papers she is grading)* **I'm**
6   **sorry, but I don't accept late work.**
7   **CARTER: This is not an assignment.**
8   **MRS. MOORE:** *(Glances up.)* **Or bribes.**
9   **CARTER: I wasn't trying to bribe you, Mrs. Moore! Besides, I**
10   **thought teachers liked apples.**
11   **MRS. MOORE: Maybe in elementary school they do.**
12   **CARTER: But it's the thought that counts, right?**
13   **MRS. MOORE:** *(Flips open a grade book.)* **Carter, let's see what**
14   **your average is in my class.** *Ah ha!* **Just as I thought!**
15   **CARTER: Low C?**
16   **MRS. MOORE: Try low D.**
17   **CARTER: I know, I know. I'm terrible in English.**
18   **MRS. MOORE: No, you're terrible at paying attention in my**
19   **class. Half the grade is for your classroom work. And how**
20   **hard is that? All I do is check your notebook for your essay**
21   **entries and you get an easy hundred for that. And how**
22   **many times have I told my students that if you complete**
23   **your assignments on time there is no way you will fail my**
24   **class?**
25   **CARTER: Mrs. Moore, I think I have A.D.D.**
26   **MRS. MOORE: Oh, and have you seen a physician for this? Are**

1 you on medication?

2 CARTER: No, but when my mom sees my report card next week

3 I'm sure she'll do something drastic.

4 MRS. MOORE: Perhaps a good swift kick in the pants would be

5 more helpful.

6 CARTER: So, you don't want my apple?

7 MRS. MOORE: An apple? Are you serious? Carter, are you

8 attempting to get on my good side?

9 CARTER: Well, I ...

10 MRS. MOORE: Because if you are, let me enlighten you. I don't

11 like apples! Never have, never will!

12 CARTER: Oh. I'm sorry, Mrs. Moore. I didn't know. *(Drops apple*

13 *in a nearby trash can.)*

14 MRS. MOORE: But chocolate ... I *love* chocolate! Milk chocolate,

15 dark chocolate, white chocolate, chocolate with nuts,

16 chocolate without ... any kind of chocolate! Oh, my mouth

17 is watering at just the thought of it!

18 CARTER: So I should bring you some chocolate instead?

19 MRS. MOORE: If you want to get on my good side.

20 CARTER: I do!

21 MRS. MOORE: Then no apples! Chocolate! Oh, if I didn't have

22 to stay in this classroom, I'd run to the candy machine

23 right now and get a chocolate bar! Hint, hint!

24 CARTER: I could go get you one!

25 MRS. MOORE: Really? And what would you expect from me if I

26 accepted your candy bar?

27 CARTER: Nothing. Well, I mean ... if you could help me bring

28 my grade up. I mean ... maybe a little tutoring or

29 something.

30 MRS. MOORE: And how often could you bring chocolate to my

31 classroom?

32 CARTER: Every day if you wanted me to!

33 MRS. MOORE: Let's see ... and you'll start completing your daily

34 assignments?

35 CARTER: Yes, ma'am!

1   MRS. MOORE: And bring me chocolate every day?

2   CARTER: Yes, ma'am!

3   MRS. MOORE: *(Looks in the grade book.)* Well, what do you

4   know! I looked at the wrong grade earlier. You do have a

5   low C after all!

6   CARTER: Great! That's great!

7   MRS. MOORE: Carter, aren't you forgetting something?

8   CARTER: Thank you! Thank you so much!

9   MRS. MOORE: Not that! My chocolate!

10 CARTER: Oh! Oh yeah! I'll go to the candy machine right now

11   and get you a chocolate bar! *(Runs out, then quickly runs*

12   *back in.)* Mrs. Moore, can I borrow a dollar?

49. Sweet Dreams

Cast: CHASE, OLIVIA
Props: Cell phone, books.
Setting: A classroom.

1   *(AT RISE: CHASE and OLIVIA are sitting at desks in a*
2   *classroom. CHASE has his head down, sleeping. He begins to*
3   *snore.)*
4   **OLIVIA:** *(Shaking his arm)* **Wake up!** *(He moans. She shakes his*
5   *arm again.)* **Wake up! Your snoring is interferring with my**
6   **concentration!**
7   **CHASE:** *(Yawning, stretching)* **I was snoring?**
8   **OLIVIA: Yes! And if we didn't have a sub today, you'd be in**
9   **trouble!**
10   **CHASE: Yeah, well, I'm tired. And the sub doesn't care. She's**
11   **reading some romance novel. Wake me up when the bell**
12   **rings, OK?**
13   **OLIVIA: Waking you up is not my job, Chase! Sorry.**
14   **CHASE: It was a minute ago.**
15   **OLIVIA: Because you were snoring and I couldn't think.**
16   **CHASE: You're lying. I don't snore.**
17   **OLIVIA: Believe me, you snore. Like this.** *(She imitates.)*
18   **CHASE: Olivia, maybe you snore like that, but I don't.**
19   **OLIVIA: Then go back to sleep and I'll record you on my cell**
20   **phone and prove it to you.**
21   **CHASE: Whatever.** *(Lays his head down.)*
22   **OLIVIA: Whatever!** *(Goes back to working on an assignment.*
23   *After a moment, he begins snoring again. She takes out her*
24   *cell phone and records him. Afterwards, she shakes his arm.)*
25   **Wake up! Hey! Wake up!**
26   **CHASE:** *(Startled, he grabs his books and stands.)* **What? Did the**

1   bell ring?

2   OLIVIA: No.

3   CHASE: *(Looks around.)* **Oh.** *(Sits down.)* **Then why did you wake**

4   **me up?**

5   OLIVIA: Because you were snoring.

6   CHASE: I told you, Olivia, I don't snore!

7   OLIVIA: Oh, yes you do!

8   CHASE: No I don't!

9   OLIVIA: *(Smiling)* **Got it recorded right here.**

10   CHASE: Let me see that!

11   OLIVIA: *(Holding the phone out, she shows him.)* **Can you hear**

12   **that? Want me to turn up the volume?**

13   CHASE: So what? I bet you snore!

14   OLIVIA: I do not! Only guys snore.

15   CHASE: Not true. My grandmother snores louder than my

16   grandfather.

17   OLIVIA: Well, that's because she's old.

18   CHASE: I'm going back to sleep. I'm tired. And don't wake me

19   up. *(Lays his head down.)*

20   OLIVIA: Then don't snore! *(She goes back to her assignment.)*

21   CHASE: *(After a moment, he begins talking in his sleep.)* **No!**

22   **Don't! Stop it! I don't like shots! No! Don't! It's going to**

23   **hurt! Mommy! Mommy!**

24   OLIVIA: Mommy? *(Leans over.)* **Is this a joke or are you really**

25   **dreaming?**

26   CHASE: Mommy! Mommy, don't let them hurt me! No,

27   mommy!

28   OLIVIA: Chase, I know you're doing this as a joke. I'm not

29   laughing.

30   CHASE: No, mommy! No!

31   OLIVIA: You're getting on my nerves, Chase!

32   CHASE: I'm scared! I'm scared, mommy!

33   OLIVIA: *(Shake his arm.)* **Would you stop it! Stop it!**

34   CHASE: *(Sits up, looking around.)* **What? What? Did the bell**

35   **ring?**

1   **OLIVIA: Chase, you know the bell didn't ring.**

2   **CHASE: Then why did you wake me up?**

3   **OLIVIA: I didn't wake you up. You were just being stupid.**

4   **CHASE: Was I snoring again?**

5   **OLIVIA: No! You were talking in your sleep!**

6   **CHASE: No I wasn't. I don't talk in my sleep.**

7   **OLIVIA: If that wasn't a joke, then you are really weird!**

8   *(Laughs, imitates him.)* **"Mommy! Mommy! Help me,**

9   **Mommy!"**

10 **CHASE: That's not funny, Olivia!**

11 **OLIVIA:** *(Imitates him.)* **"Mommy, I don't like shots! Don't let**

12   **them hurt me!"**

13 **CHASE: I didn't say that!**

14 **OLIVIA: Oh, yes you did! You were crying out for your mommy!**

15 **CHASE: Whatever!**

16 **OLIVIA: It's true.**

17 **CHASE: Leave me alone. I'm going back to sleep. And this time,**

18   **don't wake me up!** *(Lays his head down.)*

19 **OLIVIA:** *(She glares at him as he goes back to sleep. After a*

20   *moment, she stands and gathers her books.)* **Gosh, it's too**

21   **bad you didn't hear the bell ring. Sweet dreams.** *(She*

22   *exits.)*

23 **CHASE:** *(In his sleep)* **Mommy ... Mommy ...**

50. Text Me

Cast: DYLAN, MARIA
Props: Pen and paper.
Setting: School hallway.

1   (AT RISE: As MARIA is walking down the hall, DYLAN runs
2   after her.)
3 DYLAN: Maria, wait up! Wait up! (Trying to catch his breath)
4 MARIA: Dylan, why are you running down the hall, screaming
5   out my name?
6 DYLAN: (Still trying to catch his breath) Because ... because ...
7   because ...
8 MARIA: Because?
9 DYLAN: Because I wanted to ask you something!
10 MARIA: Then why didn't you just send me a text message?
11 DYLAN: Because I don't have your number.
12 MARIA: Oh.
13 DYLAN: And besides, what I wanted to ask you, well, it's not
14   really appropriate for a text message.
15 MARIA: Well, you're here now, so why don't you ask me?
16 DYLAN: (Takes a deep breath.) OK. (Clears throat.) Maria, would
17   you go to the Homecoming Dance with me?
18 MARIA: Dylan, you should have sent me a text.
19 DYLAN: I told you, I didn't have your number.
20 MARIA: Then why didn't you ask me for my number?
21 DYLAN: Why? You'd rather me ask you to the Homecoming
22   Dance via text message?
23 MARIA: Well, it would be less embarrassing.
24 DYLAN: For who? You or me?
25 MARIA: You.
26 DYLAN: I'm not embarrassed.

1   MARIA: OK, well, less humiliating.

2   DYLAN: I'm not humiliated. Unless of course you're about to

3   turn me down. Then I might be. Is that what you're going

4   to do?

5   MARIA: I'd rather just send you my answer through a text, OK?

6   DYLAN: It's a no, isn't it?

7   MARIA: Sorry.

8   DYLAN: Oh. Can I ask why?

9   MARIA: Why?

10 DYLAN: Because I want to know.

11 MARIA: Dylan, I'd rather just text you why.

12 DYLAN: I'm standing right here, Maria. I can take it.

13 MARIA: Are you sure?

14 DYLAN: Yep.

15 MARIA: Well, the truth is ... *(Pause)*

16 DYLAN: Go ahead, Maria. I can handle the truth.

17 MARIA: Which is what I'm trying to tell you!

18 DYLAN: OK, tell me.

19 MARIA: Dylan, are you sure you don't want me to just text you

20   instead?

21 DYLAN: No, tell me. Really, it's OK.

22 MARIA: OK.

23 DYLAN: OK.

24 MARIA: Are you ready?

25 DYLAN: I'm ready.

26 MARIA: Well, the reason is ...

27 DYLAN: The reason is ...?

28 MARIA: I don't like you.

29 DYLAN: What? Why not?

30 MARIA: Why not?

31 DYLAN: Yes, why not! I mean, what's wrong with me? I'm

32   smart. I'm cute. I'm funny. Isn't that what all the girls

33   want in a guy? Smart, cute, and funny?

34 MARIA: How about irritating and pushy?

35 DYLAN: You think I'm irritating and pushy?

1   MARIA: You want the truth?

2   DYLAN: Yes. I mean no! I mean, not your truth!

3   MARIA: Fine.

4   DYLAN: And I think you should change your mind and say yes

5   and go to the dance with me.

6   MARIA: But I already said no. Sorry.

7   DYLAN: Because after you go out with me, you'll see what

8   you've been missing.

9   MARIA: No thanks.

10 DYLAN: Why not? Come on, Maria!

11 MARIA: Dylan, can I have your phone number?

12 DYLAN: So you can call me? Sure. *(Writes down the number and*

13   *hands it to her.)*

14 MARIA: No, so I can text you.

15 DYLAN: That you changed your mind about going with me to

16   the dance?

17 MARIA: You'll see! Gotta go! I'll text you! Bye! *(She exits.)*

18 DYLAN: *(As he stands there alone)* I don't think I'm irritating

19   and pushy. I think I'm smart, cute, and funny. *(Smiles,*

20   *looking her direction.)* OK, see you! Text me! *(He exits.)*

51. Big Fat Zero

Cast: WILLIAM, MRS. PRUITT
Props: Letter, messy notebook.
Setting: A classroom.

1 *(AT RISE: WILLIAM is standing nervously in front of MRS.*
2 *PRUITT's desk.)*
3 **MRS. PRUITT:** William, I want you to give this letter to your
4 parents.
5 **WILLIAM:** Uh-oh. What is it?
6 **MRS. PRUITT:** I need to have a conference with your parents
7 about your grades.
8 **WILLIAM:** Uh-oh.
9 **MRS. PRUITT:** And I want that note signed and returned to my
10 class tomorrow.
11 **WILLIAM:** Signed, huh?
12 **MRS. PRUITT:** Signed. And I'll be expecting a phone call from
13 your parents as well.
14 **WILLIAM:** Uh ... by the way, Mrs. Pruitt, what's my average in
15 your class?
16 **MRS. PRUITT:** Zero.
17 **WILLIAM:** Zero? Are you kidding me? *Zero?*
18 **MRS. PRUITT:** Mr. Johnson, since school started, you have yet to
19 turn in any of your assignments.
20 **WILLIAM:** But I did them!
21 **MRS. PRUITT:** Then why didn't I receive them?
22 **WILLIAM:** I don't know! I'm sure I turned them in! I mean, I
23 think I turned them in. *(Digs inside a messy notebook.)*
24 Wow. *(Small laugh)* Guess I didn't turn them in. But I
25 meant to! And see, I did the assignments!
26 **MRS. PRUITT:** *(Takes the papers and looks at them.)* And this all

1   seems to be correct.

2   WILLIAM: I knew it! Whew!

3   MRS. PRUITT: However, because you did not turn in your work,

4   your average is still a zero.

5   WILLIAM: What? But ... but!

6   MRS. PRUITT: Everyone else managed to turn in their work.

7   WILLIAM: But ... but ... I did it! And I thought I turned it in! I

8   meant to!

9   MRS. PRUITT: Mr. Johnson, this is not kindergarten. It's high

10   school.

11   WILLIAM: I know, but ... but can't you give me a break? Just this

12   once? Because if you can't, the life that I know right now

13   will end!

14   MRS. PRUITT: Yes, consequences can be painful.

15   WILLIAM: There will be no more car, cell phone, computer, TV

16   ... anything!

17   MRS. PRUITT: Then perhaps you will have learned a valuable

18   lesson.

19   WILLIAM: But I've learned my lesson! Really! Just the thought

20   of being grounded for the rest of my life has opened my

21   eyes! I swear, Mrs. Pruitt, I will never, ever fail to turn in

22   my homework late again! I promise! Cross my heart!

23   MRS. PRUITT: And ... you need a lesson in organization. Look at

24   that notebook!

25   WILLIAM: You're right! In fact, I'll clean it out right now just to

26   show you my sincerity! *(Holds notebook up and lets all the*

27   *loose papers fall out.)* Trash, trash, keep. Trash, trash, turn

28   in. Keep. Trash. Trash. Trash. Oh! There's my code of

29   conduct form! I was supposed to turn that in the first

30   week of school. Oops. Trash, trash, trash. Oh! There's my

31   locker number! I was looking for that. Turn in. Turn in.

32   Trash.

33   MRS. PRUITT: Mr. Johnson, did your parents not teach you how

34   to be more responsible?

35   WILLIAM: Oh, they taught me, but I'm just a slow learner. But

1   not anymore! I've learned my lesson! Trash, trash, trash ...
2   Oh, was I supposed to turn this in? *(Hands MRS. PRUITT a*
3   *piece of paper.)*
4   MRS. PRUITT: This was due last Friday.
5   WILLIAM: Oops. But look! I'm getting organized!
6   MRS. PRUITT: All this in just the first six weeks of school? How
7   is that possible?
8   WILLIAM: I guess I'm a messy person. My mom says I'm a pig.
9   But believe me, my messy days are over! Trash. Trash.
10   Trash. I'm turning my life around, Mrs. Pruitt!
11 MRS. PRUITT: That's good. But it still doesn't take care of the
12   zero in my class.
13 WILLIAM: *(Grabs her hand.)* Mrs. Pruitt, please ... please give
14   me another chance! And just think, it's because of you
15   that I've turned my life around!
16 MRS. PRUITT: That's being a bit dramatic.
17 WILLIAM: No, really! If you hadn't brought it to my attention
18   that I was accidentally not turning in my papers, I
19   wouldn't have realized the seriousness of my ways! Oh,
20   Mrs. Pruitt, please, please give me another chance!
21 MRS. PRUITT: OK, here's what I'm willing to do. This one time,
22   and I do mean *one time*, I will accept your late work. But
23   you must understand that it's an automatic twenty-five
24   points off each paper.
25 WILLIAM: OK, OK, that's fine!
26 MRS. PRUITT: And if this ever happens again ...
27 WILLIAM: It will never happen again, Mrs. Pruitt! I promise!
28 MRS. PRUITT: But if it does, I will be speaking to your parents.
29 WILLIAM: Yes, ma'am!
30 MRS. PRUITT: All right, now give me that note back.
31 WILLIAM: What note?
32 MRS. PRUITT: That note I was going to have you give to your
33   parents.
34 WILLIAM: *(Searching)* The note. The note. It has to be
35   somewhere!

1   **MRS. PRUITT: Did you lose that, too?**
2   **WILLIAM:** *(Looking through mounds of papers)* **I know it has to**
3   **be here somewhere! Where is that note? Where are you,**
4   **note?**

52. The Locker

Cast: COLIN, AMANDA
Props: Several schoolbooks, paper, notebook.
Setting: Hallway.

1   *(AT RISE: COLIN is following behind AMANDA, carrying*
2   *several books.)*
3   **AMANDA:** Thanks for carrying my books, Colin.
4   **COLIN:** Amanda, would you hurry up and find your locker?
5   **AMANDA:** Hold on. Hold on.
6   **COLIN:** How much further?
7   **AMANDA:** *(Flipping through her notebook)* Hold on while I find
8   my locker number.
9   **COLIN:** You don't know where your locker is?
10 **AMANDA:** Colin, this is the first day of school! I've never been
11   to my locker before. That's why I need to find my locker
12   number.
13 **COLIN:** Then why am I following you down the hall when you
14   don't even know where it is?
15 **AMANDA:** Because I had to stop and say hi to Mrs. Brady first. I
16   had her for Science last year and she's my favorite teacher.
17 **COLIN:** You're making small talk while I'm dying here?
18 **AMANDA:** Colin, you're the best boyfriend ever. Did I say thank
19   you for carrying my books?
20 **COLIN:** Amanda, can we stop talking and find your locker?
21   Please?
22 **AMANDA:** Hold on. Hold on. Let me find it. *(Still looking*
23   *through her notebook)* Oh, here's my permission slip for
24   traveling during the school year. I need to have my
25   parents sign that tonight. And here's the combination
26   number for my band locker. And my schedule. Oh, and

1 look! My math teacher, Mr. Hernandez, gave out this
2 worksheet of, like, a million problems to do by tomorrow!
3 And it's only the first day of school! Can you believe that?
4 COLIN: I'm in pain here!
5 AMANDA: What is wrong with you?
6 COLIN: These books weigh at least a hundred pounds!
7 AMANDA: Oh, oh, sorry! I was looking for my locker number,
8 wasn't I?
9 COLIN: Hurry up!
10 AMANDA: Where did I put it?
11 COLIN: You found everything else! Why can't you find your
12 locker number?
13 AMANDA: Because it was such a small piece of paper. Hold on.
14 I'm looking.
15 COLIN: Hurry up!
16 AMANDA: Hold on. Hold on. I'm looking.
17 COLIN: If you can't find it, maybe you should just take your
18 books home tonight.
19 AMANDA: No way! I'm not carrying all those books home
20 tonight, then back to school tomorrow. I'm not that
21 strong!
22 COLIN: Neither am I, Amanda! I can't even feel my arms
23 anymore.
24 AMANDA: Then why don't you set them down while I look for
25 my locker number?
26 COLIN: *(Sets the books down. Shakes out arms.)* All this time I
27 thought I was following you to your locker.
28 AMANDA: Well, I'm sorry. I can't find my locker number.
29 COLIN: *(Sits on the books.)* Then maybe you should go to the
30 office and ask for it.
31 AMANDA: Hold on. I'll find it. Not here. Or here. Where can it
32 be?
33 COLIN: I say we go to the office.
34 AMANDA: Wait. Let me check my pockets. *(Checks pants*
35 *pockets.)* Oh, here it is! OK, come on, let's go.

1   COLIN: I don't know if I can.

2   AMANDA: Sure you can. Here, let me help you.

3   COLIN: *(Picks up a few books.)* **OK, you take half and I'll take**
4   **half.**

5   AMANDA: *(Stacks the remaining books onto his stack.)* **Here you**
6   **go.**

7   COLIN: **What about your half?**

8   AMANDA: **My half? I'm not carrying those books!**

9   COLIN: **How far do we have to go?**

10   AMANDA: *(Looking at the piece of paper)* **Locker number three-**
11   **ninety-two. Third floor.**

12   COLIN: *Third floor?*

13   AMANDA: **Come on.** *(He doesn't move.)* **Come on, Colin!**

14   COLIN: **Couldn't you take half?**

15   AMANDA: **Me?**

16   COLIN: **No, the janitor! Who else, Amanda?**

17   AMANDA: **I thought we already went over this! Colin, you're my**
18   **boyfriend, which means you're supposed to carry my**
19   **books.**

20   COLIN: **Who says?**

21   AMANDA: **Who says? It's just a known rule, Colin! Come on.**
22   **Let's head up to the third floor and find my locker.**

23   COLIN: *(Sets the books down.)* **Amanda, how long have we been**
24   **going out?**

25   AMANDA: **Colin, you know how long we've been going out.**

26   COLIN: **Since sixth period! A little over an hour!**

27   AMANDA: **So?**

28   COLIN: **Well, I want to break up.**

29   AMANDA: **What? So soon? Why?**

30   COLIN: **Because going out with you is too painful.**

31   AMANDA: **But ...**

32   COLIN: *(Walking away)* **But who knows, if it's meant to be,**
33   **maybe we can get back together tomorrow ... after you've**
34   **found your locker.** *(Exits.)*

35   AMANDA: **Colin! I can't carry all these books!**

53. No Gum Allowed

Cast: AIDEN, FAITH
Props: Several copies of a petition, pen.

1 FAITH: Aiden, would you please sign this petition?

2 AIDEN: What's it for?

3 FAITH: I'm trying to get one thousand signatures.

4 AIDEN: And again I ask, what for?

5 FAITH: To convince the school to change their policy of not
6   allowing students to chew gum.

7 AIDEN: We can't?

8 FAITH: Aiden, where have you been? Rule seven eighty-seven
9   clearly states that gum is not allowed.

10 AIDEN: They have seven hundred and eighty-seven rules?
11   Dang!

12 FAITH: There are more than seven hundred and eighty-seven
13   rules, but I'm trying to have that one eradicated.

14 AIDEN: Wow. That's a big word.

15 FAITH: So, will you sign my petition?

16 AIDEN: Faith, have you ever noticed how almost everyone
17   chews gum?

18 FAITH: And if you're caught, what happens?

19 AIDEN: Well, I never get caught. But I suppose if you're caught,
20   then you have to spit it out.

21 FAITH: Exactly! And why should we be forced to spit out our
22   gum?

23 AIDEN: I don't know. Why should we be forced to go to school?
24   Or do homework? Start a petition on that! I'll sign it!

25 FAITH: My point is that chewing gum does not distract students
26   from learning.

1   AIDEN: True.

2   FAITH: In fact, it probably helps to keep us awake.

3   AIDEN: Yeah. And I like blowing these really big bubbles when

4   I'm bored. One time I got one this big ... *(Demonstrates*

5   *with his hands.)* Well, almost that big.

6   FAITH: So I ask you, what is the crime in chewing gum?

7   AIDEN: I see no crime.

8   FAITH: Then, here, sign my petition.

9   AIDEN: No problem. *(Signs.)* And I agree. Chewing gum should

10   be allowed in school. Especially since we all do it anyway.

11 FAITH: It's a ridiculous policy that needs to be changed.

12 AIDEN: Yeah. It's not like we're ten years old and we stick our

13   wad of gum in a girl's hair.

14 FAITH: Or under a desk.

15 AIDEN: Well, I might have done that a few times this year, but

16   only 'cause it lost its flavor and I didn't want to get up to

17   throw it away. Did you know that there's a ton of gum

18   under the desks? Yuck.

19 FAITH: And as stated here in my letter, chewing gum in school

20   should be allowed for multiple reasons. To boost a low

21   sugar level, fight plaque, curb hunger ...

22 AIDEN: Freshen breath!

23 FAITH: Relieve stress.

24 AIDEN: Yeah, like when you're taking a test, chomping on a big

25   wad of gum can help you think!

26 FAITH: That's true. And I read a study that shows that students

27   who chew gum during tests do twenty-six to thirty-six

28   percent better on scores.

29 AIDEN: Wow. You did your homework! And that's good because

30   you may need some of those statistics to back up your

31   petition.

32 FAITH: Aiden, would you like to help me gather up more

33   signatures?

34 AIDEN: Sure. Just give me some of your papers.

35 FAITH: *(Handing him a few sheets)* But let me warn you, if any

1   of the teachers figure out what you're trying to do, they

2   may confiscate your signed pages.

3 AIDEN: Don't worry. If I can chew gum all through elementary,

4   junior high, and high school and not get caught, then I can

5   surely get a few hundred signatures without any

6   problems. So, do you think this might actually work?

7 FAITH: I'm hoping.

8 AIDEN: And if it doesn't?

9 FAITH: Then I'll approach the school board on this matter.

10 AIDEN: Wow. You've got guts.

11 FAITH: Thank you.

12 AIDEN: Well, I've gotta get to gym class. *(Takes gum out of*

13   *mouth.)* Coach would skin me alive if he caught me

14   chewing this gum. He's afraid we're gonna drop our gum

15   on the gym floor and make a big sticky mess! Like, who'd

16   do that? *(Sticks his gum on the wall.)* Like I'd put it on the

17   gym floor! I'm not that stupid! Who wants to step on gum

18   and get it all over their shoes? Yuck. See ya. *(Exits.)*

19 FAITH: But ... but ... You didn't mean to do that, did you? Are you

20   coming back for it? Oh! *(Tears up petition and exits.)*

54. Two-Timing Pig

Cast: DRAKE, LINDA
Setting: Hallway.

1 DRAKE: Linda, we need to talk.

2 LINDA: Drake, the bell's about to ring. Can't it wait until lunch?

3 DRAKE: No. I have to tell you this now.

4 LINDA: What? What's so important?

5 DRAKE: I'm a two-timing pig.

6 LINDA: What? What are you talking about?

7 DRAKE: It's true. I'm a two-timing pig. I know you'll probably
8   hate me after this, but I have to get this off my chest.

9 LINDA: You've been cheating on me?

10 DRAKE: Like I said, I'm a pig.

11 LINDA: I can't believe this! You've been cheating on me?

12 DRAKE: Hit me. Go ahead. Hit me.

13 LINDA: Why? Why would you do this to me?

14 DRAKE: Call it a weak moment. A stupid moment.

15 LINDA: So, how long has this been going on?

16 DRAKE: Twenty-two days to be exact. And it's killing me. The
17   lies, the deceit ...

18 LINDA: So all those times you couldn't go out with me, you
19   were going out with *her*?

20 DRAKE: It's true. I lied to you. I'm a lying pig. Do you want to
21   hit me now?

22 LINDA: So why are you confessing now? So I'll get mad and
23   break up with you? So then you can put all your energies
24   into *her*?

25 DRAKE: No, no, it's not that. I just couldn't keep up with the lies
26   anymore. It was killing me.

1   LINDA: Then you're going to break it off with her?

2   DRAKE: I was, but ...

3   LINDA: But what?

4   DRAKE: But she beat me to it.

5   LINDA: Then why are you confessing if she broke up with you?

6   DRAKE: Because, well ... she found out about you and ... well,

7   you know.

8   LINDA: Oh! And now she's planning to tell me that you've been

9   cheating on me!

10 DRAKE: I wanted you to hear it from me first, Linda. I lied and

11   I'm sorry. So go ahead. If it'll make you feel better, hit me.

12 LINDA: Let me ask you this, Drake.

13 DRAKE: Anything, Linda. And I'll tell you the truth.

14 LINDA: What if she hadn't dumped you? Who would you have

15   chosen? Or would you have continued this little game?

16 DRAKE: No, no! I would have seen the light and confessed! And

17   there's no decision to make. I look at her, I look at you ...

18   and it's you! You're the only one I want!

19 LINDA: Really? Since when? Since she found out what a jerk

20   you were?

21 DRAKE: Since I had that dream last night.

22 LINDA: What dream?

23 DRAKE: OK, let me tell you about my dream. See, I was in a boat

24   and you and ... and her ... had both fallen overboard and

25   neither of you could swim.

26 LINDA: I can swim.

27 DRAKE: It was a dream, Linda. So, neither of you could swim,

28   and you were both drowning.

29 LINDA: And?

30 DRAKE: And I had to make a choice. Save you or save her.

31 LINDA: Why not save both of us?

32 DRAKE: It was a dream, Linda. I could only save one of you.

33 LINDA: And let me guess. You picked me.

34 DRAKE: No. You died.

35 LINDA: *What?*

1   DRAKE: And I cried and cried and cried. I never got over you,
2   Linda. Never!
3   LINDA: Gee, thanks, Drake. Thanks for letting me drown.
4   DRAKE: But don't you see? When she lived and you died, it
5   made sense to me then. It was *you* who I really wanted.
6   LINDA: Drake, you have weird dreams.
7   DRAKE: Linda, it's you who I want to be with. That is, if you can
8   forgive me.
9   LINDA: Brittany and I talked on the phone last night. For three
10   hours.
11 DRAKE: Uh-oh.
12 LINDA: Guess you were a little late with your confession,
13   Drake.
14 DRAKE: *(Holds out arm.)* Hit me. Go ahead. Hit me.
15 LINDA: It's funny because I had a dream last night, too.
16 DRAKE: About us running through a field of wildflowers and
17   into each other's arms?
18 LINDA: No. Me and you and Brittany were all on that boat, and
19   guess what?
20 DRAKE: What?
21 LINDA: You fell overboard, not us. And you were screaming for
22   us to save you because you couldn't swim.
23 DRAKE: But I can swim.
24 LINDA: It was a dream, Drake. A wonderful, wonderful dream.
25 DRAKE: And?
26 LINDA: You drowned.
27 DRAKE: You let me drown?
28 LINDA: We let you drown, Drake.
29 DRAKE: So you both hate me now, don't you?
30 LINDA: In a word, yes!
31 DRAKE: And you'll never forgive me?
32 LINDA: You've got that right! Oh, and Drake ... *(Punches him in
33   the stomach.)* Thanks! I did want to hit you!
34 DRAKE: *(Bent over in pain)* Linda! Linda! Can't we work this
35   out?

55. The Meanest Girl

Cast: JARED, BAILEY
Setting: Hallway.

1 **JARED:** *(Reaches out and touches BAILEY's arm as she is walking*
2   *by.)* **Could you help me?**
3 **BAILEY: Sure. What did you need?**
4 **JARED: Could you walk me to Mr. Carroll's class?**
5 **BAILEY: Walk you? You can't walk yourself?**
6 **JARED: I could, but I don't want to run into people. Or walls. Or**
7   **open lockers.**
8 **BAILEY: Why would you do that? Are you blind?**
9 **JARED: Yes. Yes, I'm blind.**
10 **BAILEY:** *(Laughs.)* **No you're not!**
11 **JARED: It's true. Usually I get to my classes just fine, but today**
12   **I got distracted. You see, normally I count out my steps.**
13   **One hundred thirty-four steps to Math. Two hundred**
14   **seventy-eight steps to Chemistry. Eighty-nine steps to the**
15   **cafeteria ...**
16 **BAILEY: Stop teasing me! You know you can see me!**
17 **JARED: I wish I could. You sound pretty.**
18 **BAILEY: And how did you supposedly get distracted?**
19 **JARED: Well, I was eavesdropping on two other students who**
20   **were talking about some girl named Bailey.**
21 **BAILEY: Bailey? Bailey who?**
22 **JARED: I don't know. I don't think they mentioned her last**
23   **name.**
24 **BAILEY: Now I know you're lying to me because my name is**
25   **Bailey! And there are not too many Baileys in this school!**
26 **JARED: I'm not lying. I promise.** *(Reaches out, searches for her*

1   *hand, then finally finds it.)* **Please ... will you walk me to Mr.**
2   **Carroll's class? It always takes me one hundred ninety-**
3   **three steps, but like I said, I got distracted and I don't**
4   **know where I'm at.**
5   **BAILEY: Then why don't you get a seeing-eye dog?**
6   **JARED: I have one, but they prefer that I not bring him to**
7   **school because they're afraid the other students will want**
8   **to play with him. His name is Scooter.**
9   **BAILEY: Scooter?**
10   **JARED: Yes.** *(Reaches out again and searches for her hand.)*
11   **Please, please help me.**
12   **BAILEY:** *(Steps away.)* **Stop it! And stop lying to me! I know you**
13   **can see me!**
14   **JARED:** *(Reaching out)* **If I could just hold onto your elbow as**
15   **you lead me to class.**
16   **BAILEY: I know! How about if I point you in the right direction**
17   **and give you a little push?**
18   **JARED: But how will I know when I reach the end of the hall**
19   **and need to turn left?**
20   **BAILEY: When you slam into the wall!**
21   **JARED: Wow. You have no sympathy for blind people, do you?**
22   **BAILEY: No, because we don't have blind people in our school!**
23   **JARED:** *(Raises hand.)* **Me. I'm blind. I know I'm not normal, but**
24   **you don't have to make fun of me.** *(Reaches out.)* **Please,**
25   **please help me.**
26   **BAILEY: Stop it! Stop teasing me!**
27   **JARED: I was up to seventy or eighty steps on my way to Mr.**
28   **Carroll's class, but like I said, I got distracted when I heard**
29   **this really interesting conversation about this girl.**
30   **BAILEY: Whose name is Bailey? Like mine?**
31   **JARED: Yes. But I'm sure it's not you. I'm sure it's another**
32   **Bailey.**
33   **BAILEY: Let's see, I think there's only one other girl in this**
34   **school with the name of Bailey, so that means it's a fifty-**
35   **fifty chance they were talking about me.**

1   JARED: **Well, this Bailey is supposed to be really cute.**

2   BAILEY: *(Smiles.)* **Oh! Then that's me!**

3   JARED: **Maybe.** *(Holds out hands as he starts to leave.)* **Well, see**

4   **ya.** *(Takes a few steps, counting.)* **One, two, three ...**

5   BAILEY: *(Grabs his arm.)* **Wait! Where are you going?**

6   JARED: **To see if I can find my way to class. Where was I? Let's**

7   **see ... One, two, three ...**

8   BAILEY: **Wait. If you'll tell me what you heard about me, then**

9   **I'll help you to class, OK?**

10 JARED: **Really?**

11 BAILEY: **Really. Now tell me!**

12 JARED: **Well, remember, it might not be you.**

13 BAILEY: **If they said she was cute, then that's me.**

14 JARED: **Why? Is the other Bailey at school ugly?**

15 BAILEY: **Terribly!**

16 JARED: **Can I touch your face?** *(Reaches out.)* **You sound pretty.**

17 BAILEY: *(Pushes his hands away.)* **Stop it and tell me what you**

18   **heard!**

19 JARED: **Are you sure you want to hear?**

20 BAILEY: **Yes!**

21 JARED: **And if I tell you, you'll walk me to Mr. Carroll's class?**

22 BAILEY: **Yes! I already told you I would! Now tell me what you**

23   **heard!**

24 JARED: **And you won't let me run into the walls?**

25 BAILEY: *(Becoming increasingly frustrated)* **No, I won't let you**

26   **run into the walls!**

27 JARED: **Thank you. Thank you so much. You do sound pretty.**

28   *(Reaches out.)* **Can I touch your hair?**

29 BAILEY: **No! Now tell me what you heard!**

30 JARED: **OK, OK. There were these two boys talking about this**

31   **pretty girl named Bailey.**

32 BAILEY: *(Smiles.)* **Me!**

33 JARED: **And one of the boys said he thought she was the**

34   **meanest girl in school.**

35 BAILEY: *What?*

1   JARED: Then the other boy said you were mean because people
2   are mean to you. Are you mean to people?
3   BAILEY: No! What else did they say?
4   JARED: Then the other boy said you wouldn't know a nice boy
5   if he fell at your feet. And the other boy said he'd die
6   before falling at your feet.
7   BAILEY: What a mean thing to say!
8   JARED: Then the other boy said he'd asked you to the prom last
9   week.
10 BAILEY: Nick? Nick was talking about me?
11 JARED: Then this guy Nick said not only had you said no, but
12   you said ...
13 BAILEY: I said, "I wouldn't go with you if you were the last
14   person on earth!"
15 JARED: That's what he said you said.
16 BAILEY: And then what?
17 JARED: Then he said any guy who wanted to take you to the
18   prom would have to be retarded or blind. *(Pause. He smiles*
19   *at her.)* I didn't want to act retarded.
20 BAILEY: I knew it! I knew you weren't blind!
21 JARED: Did it work? Do you want to go to the prom with me?
22   *(Smiles.)*
23 BAILEY: No! Absolutely not! *(Starts to leave, then turns back.)*
24   And you know what? I hope you do run into the walls!

56. Public Display of Affection

Cast: ERIC, LYNN
Setting: Hallway.

1 ERIC: You know, I can understand the teachers not allowing us
2   to kiss at school, but what's the big deal about holding
3   hands?
4 LYNN: I know! The principal was like, "If I see you holding
5   hands again, it'll be after-school detention for the both of
6   you!"
7 ERIC: That is so stupid!
8 LYNN: What's the crime in holding hands?
9 ERIC: Obviously the principal doesn't know what it's like to be
10   in love.
11 LYNN: Yeah, who would ever love him?
12 ERIC: I can't stand this!
13 LYNN: Me neither!
14 ERIC: I just want to reach out ... *(Reaches out for her.)*
15 LYNN: Me, too. *(They both reach out with their hands, but don't*
16   *touch.)* I want to hold your hand.
17 ERIC: This is cruel and unusual punishment! Who made the
18   stupid rule about no PDA.?
19 LYNN: Adults. They always have to take the fun out of
20   everything! I just don't understand. What's the big deal?
21 ERIC: I don't know. I asked Mr. Wilson that same question and
22   do you know what he said? "Boys and girls need to keep
23   their hands to themselves."
24 LYNN: That is so stupid.
25 ERIC: And you know what else isn't fair? I see Mr. Wilson giving

1   the teachers hugs. That's PDA!

2   LYNN: I know! So the principal can show a little PDA and we

3   can't?

4   ERIC: Then we should be allowed to hug!

5   LYNN: You're right! *(They smile, then hug.)*

6   ERIC: We can't get into trouble for that. *(They smile and hug*

7   *again.)*

8   LYNN: *(Pulling away)* Uh-oh.

9   ERIC: What?

10 LYNN: Mr. Wilson is right down the hall.

11 ERIC: Great! You know, these teachers are determined to make

12   our lives miserable.

13 LYNN: Step back! No PDA! Because that's a crime according to

14   Mr. Wilson!

15 ERIC: Look! Mr. Wilson is hugging Ms. Little!

16 LYNN: And that was a lot longer hug than ours!

17 ERIC: So, see! We may not be able to hold hands, but we can

18   hug!

19 LYNN: Well, knowing Mr. Wilson, I wouldn't count on it.

20 ERIC: I know. Let's walk a little closer to Mr. Wilson, give each

21   other a hug and see what happens.

22 LYNN: Good idea. *(They move across the room, look in the*

23   *direction of Mr. Wilson, then give each other a hug, both*

24   *looking his way.)* Is he looking?

25 ERIC: Staring right at us.

26 LYNN: Does he look mad?

27 ERIC: He doesn't look happy.

28 LYNN: Did he just yell at us?

29 ERIC: Smile and wave. Pretend we didn't hear him. *(They both*

30   *smile and wave in his direction.)*

31 LYNN: What was he saying?

32 ERIC: "Break it up! Break it up!"

33 LYNN: Guess hugs aren't allowed either.

34 ERIC: It's not fair! He can show a little PDA and we can't?

35 LYNN: I hate this!

1   ERIC: Me too! *(He reaches out his hand.)* **I just want to hold your**
2   **hand!**
3   LYNN: *(Reaches out, but their hands don't touch.)* **Me too! Hey,**
4   **you want to try and hold pinkies during Science class?**
5   ERIC: **You bet! That might help me get through the day.**
6   LYNN: **And hopefully we won't get into trouble.**
7   ERIC: **Yeah, for holding pinkies! Can you imagine them giving**
8   **us detention for touching pinkies?**
9   LYNN: **Knowing Mr. Wilson, he would.**
10 ERIC: **Hey, I have an idea!**
11 LYNN: **What?**
12 ERIC: *(Offers his hand.)* **It was very nice talking to you.**
13 LYNN: *(Gives his hand a long shake, smiling.)* **And it was nice**
14   **talking to you, too.**
15 ERIC: **See you in Science.**
16 LYNN: **Can't wait.**

57. Expecting Tears

Cast: SID, KIM
Props: Box of tissues.

.

1 (AT RISE: SID approaches KIM, who is holding a large box of
2 tissues.)
3 SID: Kim, why are you carrying around a box of tissues?
4 KIM: Because Matt broke up with me during first period!
5 SID: Oh. I'm sorry, Kim.
6 KIM: And he didn't even have the guts to tell me to my face! He
7 just passed me a note that said, "I want to break up. But
8 we can still be friends, can't we?" No!
9 SID: He could have at least told you to your face. That's what a
10 real man would do.
11 KIM: You're right. Which means Matt is no man! He's a coward!
12 SID: If I broke up with you ... well, in the first place, I would
13 never break up with you.
14 KIM: Really?
15 SID: Really. He was an idiot.
16 KIM: Really?
17 SID: Really. So, have you been crying all morning?
18 KIM: No, not yet. But I'm afraid it'll hit me when I least expect
19 it.
20 SID: When reality sets in?
21 KIM: Yes. (Clutching the box of tissues) Then I'll be prepared.
22 SID: How long do you think it'll take? You know, for it to sink
23 in?
24 KIM: I'm guessing during lunch.
25 SID: Why lunch?
26 KIM: Because Matt and I always ate lunch together.

1 SID: Yeah, that's probably when it'll hit you.

2 KIM: And just the thought of eating all alone and without him

3   ... well, it makes me want to cry.

4 SID: Then you should prepare yourself.

5 KIM: That's a good idea. *(Pulls out a tissue.)*

6 SID: So, imagine yourself eating alone.

7 KIM: *(Puts tissue to face.)* I'm ready.

8 SID: But instead of feeling sad, you're happy.

9 KIM: I am?

10 SID: Because you found someone else to eat lunch with you.

11 KIM: I did?

12 SID: And you're having so much fun that you don't even miss

13   him.

14 KIM: I don't?

15 SID: And it's the best lunch you've had all year.

16 KIM: It is?

17 SID: Eating, laughing ... You're on top of the world!

18 KIM: I am? But ... who am I going to eat with?

19 SID: You'll have to find someone.

20 KIM: But who?

21 SID: I'm free.

22 KIM: You are? You'd have lunch with me?

23 SID: Sure. Just call me your knight in shining armor. I'm here

24   to save you!

25 KIM: Thanks, Sid. That'll at least get me through lunch. But

26   what about after that?

27 SID: Well, you have two choices. Either you allow Matt to make

28   you feel miserable, or you do something to get him out of

29   your system.

30 KIM: Like what?

31 SID: Jump into a new relationship! It beats falling apart,

32   doesn't it?

33 KIM: Yes, but ...

34 SID: Then you must act quickly!

35 KIM: How quickly?

1 SID: The sooner the better! I'd even suggest you find your new
2   guy before school lets out today.
3 KIM: But that's a lot of pressure to find a guy so quickly. And
4   who?
5 SID: Just look around and find someone who makes you smile.
6   *(Gives her a huge smile.)*
7 KIM: You know, I do like the idea of jumping into a new
8   relationship. Avoiding the heartache, the tears ...
9 SID: And Matt will probably be devastated when he finds out
10   how quickly you were snapped up after he's dumped you!
11 KIM: You know what? You're right! You're absolutely right! This
12   idea is sounding better and better by the minute!
13 SID: Glad I could be of help.
14 KIM: You've been great!
15 SID: So, you need to find a new boyfriend. And fast! Because
16   you don't want to use all those tissues, do you?
17 KIM: No! Not even one! Here, take these. *(Hands him the box of*
18   *tissues.)*
19 SID: And if there's anything, I mean, *anything* else I can do to
20   help ...
21 KIM: Thanks, but I know exactly who I'm going after!
22 SID: *(Smiling)* Really? Who?
23 KIM: *(In a dreamy tone)* Justin. *(Points.)* He's standing right over
24   there.
25 SID: But ...
26 KIM: And he's always flirting with me! All I need to do is let him
27   know I'm available. We'll probably be going steady by fifth
28   period.
29 SID: But ...
30 KIM: And thanks, Sid! Thanks so much for your helping me!
31   *(Happily, she exits.)*
32 SID: But ... but ... *(Pulls out a tissue)* I was available!

58. Mathematically Challenged

Cast: CHAD, MEGAN

1   CHAD: Megan, why are you in such a bad mood today?

2   MEGAN: Because Mr. Cone embarrassed me during Math class!

3   CHAD: What happened?

4   MEGAN: In front of the entire class he told me that I wasn't

5   going to pass Math if I didn't get the basics down!

6   CHAD: Which basics? Solving equations? That's easy. And

7   here's something I like to remember that I learned in Pre-

8   Algebra class. To solve complex equations, the one thing

9   to remember is that you need to get the variable isolated

10   before you can solve the equation. That's really important.

11   And don't forget, when you're dealing with fractions and

12   decimals, you have to be very careful with your

13   multiplication and division.

14 MEGAN: What did you just say? Oh, never mind!

15 CHAD: Megan, it's not that hard.

16 MEGAN: Well, it's hard for me, Chad!

17 CHAD: What are you having such a hard time with?

18 MEGAN: For one, my multiplication tables.

19 CHAD: Uh, Megan, we learned that in third grade.

20 MEGAN: Well, I guess I was absent, Chad! Because except for

21   my zeros and ones I can't remember them!

22 CHAD: You're kidding, right?

23 MEGAN: Do I look like I'm kidding?

24 CHAD: OK, what's six times two?

25 MEGAN: Hold on. (*She thinks for a minute, then turns from him*

26   *and counts on her fingers.*) **Twelve.**

1 CHAD: You've got to be joking! You don't know it like that?
2   *(Snaps.)*
3 MEGAN: Now you're starting to sound like Mr. Cone! Oh, I hate
4   math!
5 CHAD: Five times five?
6 MEGAN: *(Using her fingers, she counts.)* Five, ten, fifteen,
7   twenty, twenty-five. Twenty-five.
8 CHAD: Megan, by the time you're in high school, or even junior
9   high, you shouldn't be using your fingers to count.
10 MEGAN: Maybe not, but it helps!
11 CHAD: Three times two?
12 MEGAN: Hold on.
13 CHAD: Come on, don't you at least know that one?
14 MEGAN: *(Counting with her fingers.)* I was just double-
15   checking. It's six.
16 CHAD: Wow. You're right. You are terrible in Math.
17 MGAN: I told you I was. And Mr. Cone told the entire class!
18 CHAD: Well, here's what I think you should do. Go to the store
19   and buy some of those multiplication cards. You know,
20   the ones we used in elementary school. Then, you need to
21   memorize them.
22 MEGAN: Yuck! I don't want to do that!
23 CHAD: Do you want to fail math?
24 MEGAN: No, I just want to be able to use a calculator, but Mr.
25   Cone won't let us do that!
26 CHAD: Megan, you can't work out difficult math problems
27   without memorizing your multiplication tables.
28 MEGAN: I know! But I don't think it's going to work because I
29   have a mental block when it comes to numbers.
30 CHAD: Come on, Megan. You can do it. OK, what's one times
31   two?
32 MEGAN: One. Duh!
33 CHAD: Uh, that was wrong.
34 MEGAN: What?
35 CHAD: It's two. The answer is two.

1   MEGAN: See! See, I told you! I'm terrible at math! And when I
2   get out of school, I'll never do it again!
3   CHAD: But what if you go to the store? And say you have twenty
4   dollars to spend, and you want to buy three items that cost
5   seven dollars each? You'll have to figure it out in your
6   head if you can afford to buy all three.
7   MEGAN: If I had twenty dollars and the three items were seven
8   dollars each, I'd have enough money.
9   CHAD: How? Are you going to turn around and ask the
10   customer behind you if you can borrow a dollar?
11   MEGAN: *(Gives him a strange look, then counts with her fingers,*
12   *realizing she wouldn't have enough money.)* No, I was going
13   to charge it on my credit card!
14   CHAD: But what if your credit card has a limit on how much
15   you can spend.
16   MEGAN: Well, it won't!
17   CHAD: But what if it does?
18   MEGAN: Then I guess my credit card won't go through and I
19   won't get those three items I wanted!
20   CHAD: But wouldn't it be much easier to learn what seven
21   times three is?
22   MEGAN: But you don't understand! I hate, hate, hate math!
23   CHAD: Megan, you can learn this.
24   MEGAN: But it's hard!
25   CHAD: How about if I help you?
26   MEGAN: You'd lose your patience and choke me!
27   CHAD: No, no, I can handle this. One times one?
28   MEGAN: One! Duh!
29   CHAD: Good, good. One times five?
30   MEGAN: Five. Chad, I told you I knew my ones!
31   CHAD: And five times five?
32   MEGAN: Hold on. *(Counts with fingers.)*
33   CHAD: *(Grabs her hand.)* Megan, we already did this one,
34   remember? Think!
35   MEGAN: Uh ...

1 CHAD: Five times five?

2 MEGAN: Uh ...

3 CHAD: When I say five times five, think of a quarter.

4 MEGAN: George Washington!

5 CHAD: No Megan, the amount of the quarter.

6 MEGAN: Uh, Chad, a quarter is ... a quarter.

7 CHAD: And how many pennies does it take to make a quarter?

8 MEGAN: Hold on.

9 CHAD: Megan, come on!

10 MEGAN: Hold on! I'm thinking! *(After a pause)* Twenty-five
11   pennies!

12 CHAD: So, five times five is?

13 MEGAN: Twenty-five pennies!

14 CHAD: You know what? You're right!

15 MEGAN: About what?

16 CHAD: About me losing my patience and choking you! *(Exits.)*

17 MEGAN: Hey, where are you going? I thought you were going
18   to help me!

59. Extra Credit

Cast: TONY, ANGIE

Props: School picture, backpack, digital camera.

1   *(AT RISE: ANGIE rushes up to TONY, waving one of her*
2   *school pictures.)*
3   **ANGIE: Tony, do you want one of my school pictures?**
4   **TONY: Uh, sure. Thanks.**
5   **ANGIE: Can I have one of yours?**
6   **TONY: Oh, well ... I, uh, ran out. Sorry.**
7   **ANGIE: Then could I take your picture?** *(Digs in her backpack for*
8   *a digital camera.)*
9   **TONY: What? Take my picture?**
10   **ANGIE:** *(Holds up the camera.)* **With my digital camera!**
11   **TONY: No, I don't think so. I don't really like having my picture**
12   **taken.**
13   **ANGIE: Smile!** *(Takes his picture.)* **Now, let me get a couple**
14   **more. Now this time, smile! OK, the serious look. That's**
15   **OK, too.** *(Takes another picture.)*
16   **TONY: Excuse me; I didn't say you could take my picture!**
17   **ANGIE:** *(Looking at camera)* **These are great! And I'm going to**
18   **use this one as my desktop. That way I can see you all the**
19   **time.**
20   **TONY: Set me as your desktop?**
21   **ANGIE: And screensaver!**
22   **TONY: Look, I really wish you wouldn't.**
23   **ANGIE: Why not?**
24   **TONY: Because other people might see me on your computer**
25   **and get the wrong impression.**
26   **ANGIE: Wouldn't that be great? Well, at least for me!**

1 TONY: I'm sorry, but I don't feel comfortable with this. Could
2   you just erase those pictures?
3 ANGIE: *(Clutching the camera tightly)* No! Never!
4 TONY: If we were going out, it'd be different, but ...
5 ANGIE: Do you want to go out?
6 TONY: No!
7 ANGIE: Why not?
8 TONY: Because ... because I don't believe in it.
9 ANGIE: That doesn't make sense.
10 TONY: We're too young to date. We need to concentrate on our
11   education.
12 ANGIE: Weren't you dating Riley last week? You know, you have
13   a reputation for dating all the girls. And I'm a girl!
14 TONY: I know, but ...
15 ANGIE: Can I take a couple more pictures? Maybe even one or
16   two of us? *(Moves beside him and holds out camera.)*
17 TONY: *(Steps away.)* No! Look, I don't want to hurt your feelings,
18   but ...
19 ANGIE: Then let me take our picture! *(Tries again, but he*
20   *moves.)*
21 TONY: And I don't want you using my picture as your desktop
22   background or screensaver!
23 ANGIE: Oh! Oh! And there's this website where you can
24   download pictures! And for seventeen dollars you can
25   order a poster of anything you want! I might just order
26   one of you!
27 TONY: No!
28 ANGIE: It's only seventeen dollars. Then I could get one of
29   those poster frames and hang you in my room!
30 TONY: No! Are you nuts?
31 ANGIE: What's the problem? Oh, wait! I know! You don't want
32   to make your current girlfriend jealous?
33 TONY: I don't have a current girlfriend right now, but ...
34 ANGIE: Perfect. Then she won't be jealous.
35 TONY: Don't you think this is a bit obsessive?

1   ANGIE: No. So, can I get a couple more pictures? Please? I'm
2   really excited about that poster! I may even get more than
3   one.
4   TONY: Don't you get it? If you do that, it'll look like I'm your
5   boyfriend!
6   ANGIE: *(Smiling)* I know.
7   TONY: But I'm not your boyfriend, and I never will be!
8   ANGIE: I can pretend, can't I?
9   TONY: Well, why don't you get a real boyfriend? Then you won't
10   have to pretend. And I'm sure he'd let you take all the
11   pictures you want of him. Plaster your walls with him.
12   He'll appreciate that.
13 ANGIE: Maybe someday you'll appreciate it.
14 TONY: I don't think so.
15 ANGIE: Yes. When you open your eyes and stop fighting for
16   what's meant to be.
17 TONY: What's meant to be?
18 ANGIE: Us! Our desire to be together!
19 TONY: I'm not fighting that! Believe me!
20 ANGIE: *(Takes another picture.)* Yes you are. But that's OK. I'm
21   willing to wait for you to come to your senses.
22 TONY: You want to take my picture? Well, take one of this! Me
23   glaring at you!
24 ANGIE: That's cute! *(Takes his picture.)* Thanks.
25 TONY: Have you ever heard of harassment? You know, I could
26   go to the office and turn you in!
27 ANGIE: Have you ever heard of a joke?
28 TONY: A joke? This is a joke?
29 ANGIE: Kinda. I'm doing this for my psychology class. And you
30   were my lucky victim.
31 TONY: Lucky victim? But why me?
32 ANGIE: Because you're cute. *(Holds up camera.)* One more, OK?
33 TONY: *(Forces a smile.)* For an assignment?
34 ANGIE: Yes, so I can write about your reaction to me harassing
35   you. It's for a major grade.

1   **TONY: And the pictures?**

2   **ANGIE: Extra credit.**

3   **TONY: Bonus points on your paper?**

4   **ANGIE: Not exactly.**

5   **TONY: Then what's the extra credit for?**

6   **ANGIE:** *(Looking at the pictures in her camera, smiling)* **For me.**

60. Tattletale

Cast: JEFF, GINA

1   JEFF: Gina, thanks for telling Mom that I slept through first
2   period yesterday.
3   GINA: No problem, little brother. The way I see it, if I have to be
4   here, you have to be here.
5   JEFF: And why do you care? Do you not have anything better to
6   do than watch my every move then go tattletale to mom?
7   GINA: As a matter of fact, I was paying you back for digging
8   through my backpack and "accidentally" showing mom
9   my English paper.
10 JEFF: Hey, I needed to borrow some notebook paper and it fell
11   out.
12 GINA: And I needed to tell mom that you skipped first period.
13 JEFF: The school would have told her, Gina.
14 GINA: Yes, eventually. But I was happy to beat them to it.
15 JEFF: You know what, let's just pretend that we don't know
16   each other.
17 GINA: That's fine with me. You stay out of my way and out of
18   my things, and I'll do the same.
19 JEFF: But remember, you still have to give me a ride home from
20   school.
21 GINA: No, I don't think so. You can walk or, better yet, mooch a
22   ride from one of your friends.
23 JEFF: None of my friends are driving yet, Gina. And it's too far
24   to walk.
25 GINA: Then how'd you get to school yesterday after sleeping
26   through first period?

1   JEFF: I called Grandma.
2   GINA: Oh, really? And what excuse did you give Grandma for
3   needing a ride to school?
4   JEFF: I didn't have to give her an excuse. I just told her I needed
5   a ride. She doesn't ask a million questions like you do. Or
6   tattletale!
7   GINA: Then why don't you call Grandma and tell her she can
8   start giving you a ride to school and back home every day?
9   JEFF: No, Gina! Grandma has that big ole grandma car, and I
10   don't want my friends seeing me in that!
11 GINA: *(Pats his shoulder.)* Well, you'll think of something. And
12   remember, I don't know you and you don't know me.
13 JEFF: Fine! But you need to know me on the way to school and
14   on the way home.
15 GINA: No thank you. I prefer not knowing you at all.
16 JEFF: Fine then! Then I'll just tell Mom!
17 GINA: You know what? You are such a big fat baby and a big fat
18   tattletale!
19 JEFF: Learned it from you!
20 GINA: Is that what you're going to do? Run to Mommy every
21   time you don't get your way?
22 JEFF: No, just every time I can get you into trouble.
23 GINA: Well, that works both ways, little brother!
24 JEFF: Yep. So, you need to give me a ride home after school.
25 GINA: Sure, then I'll tell Mom how you wore those jeans to
26   school that she said were to go to the dumpster or be saved
27   for yard work.
28 JEFF: You are such a brat!
29 GINA: *(Smiles.)* I know.
30 JEFF: Maybe we could call a truce.
31 GINA: Nah.
32 JEFF: You do what you want and I do what I want and no more
33   running to Mom.
34 GINA: Nah. I like running to Mom. I like seeing you in trouble.
35 JEFF: OK.

1   GINA: What's this flippant OK about?

2   JEFF: Because now I'm going to be forced to tell Mom about

3   how you speed to school every morning because you're

4   looking at yourself in the mirror too long. Gosh, knowing

5   Mom, you won't be driving anymore.

6   GINA: You wouldn't!

7   JEFF: Yep. Guess Grandma will be taking us both to school

8   from now on. Oh well. See ya. *(Exits.)*

9   GINA: Wait! Wait! I do want to call a truce! Do you hear me?

10   *(Runs after him.)*

Photo by Barbara Peterson

About the Author

Laurie Allen is a West Texas playwright whose first play, *Gutter Girl*, won the Indian River Players Festival of One-Act Plays Competition. She has participated in developing original one-act plays for Hood Junior High in Odessa, Texas. Her plays have been read and produced at The Gettysburg College, the Globe of the Great Southwest, and the Pasadena Little Theatre.

Allen's plays for teens have enjoyed wide success across the United States with many productions. She has had skits, duets, and plays published by various publishing companies. Many of her competition pieces have gone all the way to national speech and forensics competitions.

Her publications include *Comedy Duets for Teens, Two-Character Scenes for Teens, Comedy Duos for Teens, Comedy Scenes for Teens,* and *Comedy Duos for High School.* Her first book, *Thirty Short Comedy Plays for Teens,* was published in 2007.

Order Form

Meriwether Publishing Ltd.
PO Box 7710
Colorado Springs, CO 80933-7710
Phone: 800-937-5297 Fax: 719-594-9916
Website: www.meriwether.com

Please send me the following books:

_____ **Sixty Comedy Duet Scenes for Teens**   **$16.95**
#BK-B302
by Laurie Allen
Real-life situations for laughter

_____ **Thirty Short Comedy Plays for Teens**   **$16.95**
#BK-B292
by Laurie Allen
Plays for a variety of cast sizes

_____ **Make It Mystery #BK-B287**   **$19.95**
by Craig Sodaro
An anthology of short mystery plays

_____ **Two-Character Plays for Student Actors**   **$16.95**
#BK-B174
by Robert Mauro
A collection of 15 one-act plays

_____ **Doubletalk — Comedy Duets for Actors**   **$15.95**
#BK-B186
by Bill Majeski
A collection of comedy duets for actors

_____ **Improv Ideas #BK-B283**   **$22.95**
by Justine Jones and Mary Ann Kelley
A book of games and lists

_____ **112 Acting Games #BK-B277**   **$17.95**
by Gavin Levy
A comprehensive workbook of theatre games

These and other fine Meriwether Publishing books are available at your local bookstore or direct from the publisher. Prices subject to change without notice. Check our website or call for current prices.

Name: _____ e-mail: _____

Organization name: _____

Address: _____

City: _____ State: _____

Zip: _____ Phone: _____

❑ **Check enclosed**

❑ **Visa / MasterCard / Discover / Am. Express #** _____

Signature: _____ *Expiration date:* _____ / _____
    (required for credit card orders)

Colorado residents: Please add 3% sales tax.
Shipping: Include $3.95 for the first book and 75¢ for each additional book ordered.

❑ *Please send me a copy of your complete catalog of books and plays.*

Order Form

Meriwether Publishing Ltd.
PO Box 7710
Colorado Springs, CO 80933-7710
Phone: 800-937-5297 Fax: 719-594-9916
Website: www.meriwether.com

Please send me the following books:

_____ **Sixty Comedy Duet Scenes for Teens**   **$16.95**
#BK-B302
by Laurie Allen
Real-life situations for laughter

_____ **Thirty Short Comedy Plays for Teens**   **$16.95**
#BK-B292
by Laurie Allen
Plays for a variety of cast sizes

_____ **Make It Mystery #BK-B287**   **$19.95**
by Craig Sodaro
An anthology of short mystery plays

_____ **Two-Character Plays for Student Actors**   **$16.95**
#BK-B174
by Robert Mauro
A collection of 15 one-act plays

_____ **Doubletalk — Comedy Duets for Actors**   **$15.95**
#BK-B186
by Bill Majeski
A collection of comedy duets for actors

_____ **Improv Ideas #BK-B283**   **$22.95**
by Justine Jones and Mary Ann Kelley
A book of games and lists

_____ **112 Acting Games #BK-B277**   **$17.95**
by Gavin Levy
A comprehensive workbook of theatre games

These and other fine Meriwether Publishing books are available at
your local bookstore or direct from the publisher. Prices subject to
change without notice. Check our website or call for current prices.

Name: _____ e-mail: _____

Organization name: _____

Address: _____

City: _____ State: _____

Zip: _____ Phone: _____

  ❏ **Check enclosed**

  ❏ **Visa / MasterCard / Discover / Am. Express #** _____

Expiration
Signature: _____ *date:* _____ / _____
    (required for credit card orders)

Colorado residents: Please add 3% sales tax.
Shipping: Include $3.95 for the first book and 75¢ for each additional book ordered.

  ❏ *Please send me a copy of your complete catalog of books and plays.*